CliffsNotes™

Shakespeare's
Macbeth

By Alex Went, M.A.

WITHDRAWN

IN THIS BOOK

- Learn about the Life and Background of the Playwright

- Preview an Introduction to the Play

- Explore themes, literary devices, and use of imagery in the Critical Commentaries

- Examine in-depth Character Analyses

- Reinforce what you learn with CliffsNotes Review

- Find additional information to further your study in the CliffsNotes Resource Center and online at www.cliffsnotes.com

IDG Books Worldwide, Inc.
An International Data Group Company
Foster City, CA • Chicago, IL • Indianapolis, IN • New York, NY

About the Author

Alex Went has been a teacher of English and Head of Drama at Shrewsbury School, England. He is the librettist of the musicals *Jekyll!*, *The Time Machine*, and *The Lost Domain*.

Publisher's Acknowledgments

Editorial

Project Editor: Tracy Barr

Acquisitions Editor: Greg Tubach

Glossary Editors: The editors and staff of Webster's New World Dictionary

Editorial Assistant: Michelle Hacker

Production

Indexer: York Production Services

Proofreader: York Production Services

CliffsNotes™ Shakespeare's *Macbeth*

Published by
IDG Books Worldwide, Inc.
An International Data Group Company
919 E. Hillsdale Blvd.
Suite 400
Foster City, CA 94404
www.idgbooks.com (IDG Books Worldwide Web site)
www.cliffsnotes.com (CliffsNotes Web site)

ISBN: 0-7645-8602-5

Printed in the United States of America

10 9 8 7 6 5 4 3 2 1

1O/RY/QV/QQ/IN

Distributed in the United States by IDG Books Worldwide, Inc.

Distributed by CDG Books Canada Inc. for Canada; by Transworld Publishers Limited in the United Kingdom; by IDG Norge Books for Norway; by IDG Sweden Books for Sweden; by IDG Books Australia Publishing Corporation Pty. Ltd. for Australia and New Zealand; by TransQuest Publishers Pte Ltd. for Singapore, Malaysia, Thailand, Indonesia, and Hong Kong; by Gotop Information Inc. for Taiwan; by ICG Muse, Inc. for Japan; by Intersoft for South Africa; by Eyrolles for France; by International Thomson Publishing for Germany, Austria and Switzerland; by Distribuidora Cuspide for Argentina; by LR International for Brazil; by Galileo Libros for Chile; by Ediciones ZETA S.C.R. Ltda. for Peru; by WS Computer Publishing Corporation, Inc., for the Philippines; by Contemporanea de Ediciones for Venezuela; by Express Computer Distributors for the Caribbean and West Indies; by Micronesia Media Distributor, Inc. for Micronesia; by Chips Computadoras S.A. de C.V. for Mexico; by Editorial Norma de Panama S.A. for Panama; by American Bookshops for Finland.

For general information on IDG Books Worldwide's books in the U.S., please call our Consumer Customer Service department at **800-762-2974**.

For reseller information, including discounts and premium sales, please call our Reseller Customer Service department at **800-434-3422**.

For information on where to purchase IDG Books Worldwide's books outside the U.S., please contact our International Sales department at **317-596-5530** or fax **317-572-4002**.

For consumer information on foreign language translations, please contact our Customer Service department at **1-800-434-3422**, fax 317-572-4002, or e-mail rights@idgbooks.com.

For information on licensing foreign or domestic rights, please phone **+1-650-653-7098**.

For sales inquiries and special prices for bulk quantities, please contact our Order Services department at **800-434-3422** or write to the address above.

For information on using IDG Books Worldwide's books in the classroom or for ordering examination copies, please contact our Educational Sales department at **800-434-2086** or fax 317-572-4005.

For press review copies, author interviews, or other publicity information, please contact our Public Relations department at **650-653-7000** or fax 650-653-7500.

For authorization to photocopy items for corporate, personal, or educational use, please contact Copyright Clearance Center, 222 Rosewood Drive, Danvers, MA 01923, or fax **978-750-4470**.

Library of Congress Cataloging-in-Publication Data

Went, Alex.
    CliffsNotes Shakespeare's Macbeth / by Alex Went.
        p. cm.
    Includes bibliographical references and index.
    ISBN 0-7645-8602-5 (alk. paper)
    1. Shakespeare, William, 1564-1616. Macbeth--Examinations--Study guides. 2. Macbeth, King of Scotland, 11th cent.--In literature. 3 Tragedy--Examinations--Study guides. I. Shakespeare's Macbeth.
PR2823.W46 2000
822.3'3.00--dc21   00-035106
                                                CIP

IDG BOOKS is a registered trademark under exclusive license to IDG Books Worldwide, Inc. from International Data Group, Inc.

Table of Contents

How to Use This Book

CliffsNotes on Shakespeare's *Macbeth* supplements the original work, giving you background information about the author, an introduction to the novel, a graphical character map, critical commentaries, expanded glossaries, and a comprehensive index. CliffsNotes Review tests your comprehension of the original text and reinforces learning with questions and answers, practice projects, and more. For further information on William Shakespeare and *Macbeth,* check out the CliffsNotes Resource Center.

CliffsNotes provides the following icons to highlight essential elements of particular interest:

Reveals the underlying themes in the work.

Helps you to more easily relate to or discover the depth of a character.

Uncovers elements such as setting, atmosphere, mystery, passion, violence, irony, symbolism, tragedy, foreshadowing, and satire.

Enables you to appreciate the nuances of words and phrases.

Don't Miss Our Web Site

Discover classic literature as well as modern-day treasures by visiting the CliffsNotes Web site at www.cliffsnotes.com. You can obtain a quick download of a CliffsNotes title, purchase a title in print form, browse our catalog, or view online samples.

You'll also find interactive tools that are fun and informative, links to interesting Web sites, tips, articles, and additional resources to help you, not only for literature, but for test prep, finance, careers, computers, and Internet too. See you at www.cliffsnotes.com!

LIFE AND BACKGROUND OF THE PLAYWRIGHT

Many books have assembled facts, reasonable suppositions, traditions, and speculations concerning the life and career of William Shakespeare. Taken as a whole, these materials give a rather comprehensive picture of England's foremost dramatic poet. Tradition and sober supposition are not necessarily false because they lack proven bases for their existence. It is important, however, that persons interested in Shakespeare should distinguish between facts and beliefs about his life.

From one point of view, modern scholars are fortunate to know as much as they do about a man of middle-class origin who left a small country town and embarked on a professional career in sixteenth-century London. From another point of view, they know surprisingly little about the writer who has continued to influence the English language and its drama and poetry for more than three hundred years. Sparse and scattered as these facts of his life are, they are sufficient to prove that a man from Stratford by the name of William Shakespeare wrote the major portion of the thirty-seven plays that scholars ascribe to him. The concise review that follows will concern itself with some of these records.

Personal History

No one knows the exact date of William Shakespeare's birth. His baptism occurred on Wednesday, April 26, 1564. His father was John Shakespeare, tanner, glover, dealer in grain, and town official of Stratford; his mother, Mary, was the daughter of Robert Arden, a prosperous gentleman-farmer. The Shakespeares lived on Henley Street.

Under a bond dated November 28, 1582, William Shakespeare and Anne Hathaway entered into a marriage contract. The baptism of their eldest child, Susanna, took place in Stratford in May, 1583. One year and nine months later their twins, Hamnet and Judith, were christened in the same church. The parents named them for the poet's friends, Hamnet and Judith Sadler.

Early in 1596, William Shakespeare, in his father's name, applied to the College of Heralds for a coat of arms. Although positive proof is lacking, there is reason to believe that the Heralds granted this request, for in 1599 Shakespeare again made application for the right to quarter his coat of arms with that of his mother. Entitled to her father's coat of arms, Mary had lost this privilege when she married John Shakespeare before he held the official status of gentleman.

In May of 1597, Shakespeare purchased New Place, the outstanding residential property in Stratford at that time. Since John Shakespeare had suffered financial reverses prior to this date, William must have achieved success for himself.

Court records show that in 1601–1602, William Shakespeare began rooming in the household of Christopher Mountjoy in London. Subsequent disputes over the wedding settlement and agreement between Mountjoy and his son-in-law, Stephen Belott, led to a series of legal actions, and in 1612 the court scribe recorded Shakespeare's deposition of testimony relating to the case. In July, 1605, William Shakespeare paid four hundred and forty pounds for the lease of a large portion of the tithes on certain real estate in and near Stratford. This was an arrangement whereby Shakespeare purchased half the annual tithes, or taxes, on certain agricultural products from parcels of land in and near Stratford. In addition to receiving approximately 10 percent income on his investment, he almost doubled his capital. This was possibly the most important and successful investment of his lifetime, and it paid a steady income for many years.

Shakespeare is next mentioned when John Combe, a resident of Stratford, died on July 12, 1614. To his friend, Combe bequeathed the sum of five pounds. These records and similar ones are important, not because of their economic significance but because they prove the existence of William Shakespeare in Stratford and in London during this period.

On March 25, 1616, William Shakespeare revised his last will and testament. He died on April 23 of the same year. His body lies within the chancel and before the altar of the Stratford church. A rather wry inscription is carved upon his tombstone:

Good Friend, for Jesus' sake, forbear

To dig the dust enclosed here;

Blest be the man that spares these bones

And curst be he who moves my bones.

The last direct descendant of William Shakespeare was his granddaughter, Elizabeth Hall, who died in 1670.

These are the most outstanding facts about Shakespeare the man, as apart from those about the dramatist and poet. Such pieces of information, scattered from 1564 through 1616, declare the existence of such a person, not as a writer or actor, but as a private citizen. It is illogical to think that anyone would or could have fabricated these details for the purpose of deceiving later generations.

His Work

In similar fashion, the evidence establishing William Shakespeare as the foremost playwright of his day is positive and persuasive. Robert Greene's *Groatsworth of Wit,* in which he attacked Shakespeare, a mere actor, for presuming to write plays in competition with Greene and his fellow playwrights, was entered in the Stationers' Register on September 20, 1592. In 1594, Shakespeare acted before Queen Elizabeth, and in 1594–1595, his name appeared as one of the shareholders of the Lord Chamberlain's Company. Francis Meres in his *Palladis Tamia* (1598) called Shakespeare "mellifluous and hony-tongued" and compared his comedies and tragedies with those of Plautus and Seneca in excellence.

Shakespeare's continued association with Burbage's company is equally definite. His name appears as one of the owners of the Globe theater in 1599. On May 19, 1603, he and his fellow actors received a patent from James I designating them as the King's Men and making them Grooms of the Chamber. Late in 1608 or early in 1609, Shakespeare and his colleagues purchased the Blackfriars Theatre and began using it as their winter location when weather made production at the Globe inconvenient.

Other specific allusions to Shakespeare and to his acting and his writing occur in numerous places. Put together, they form irrefutable testimony that William Shakespeare of Stratford and London was the leader among Elizabethan playwrights.

One of the most impressive of all proofs of Shakespeare's authorship of his plays is the First Folio of 1623, with the dedicatory verse that appeared in it. John Heminge and Henry Condell, members of Shakespeare's own company, stated that they collected and issued the plays as a memorial to their fellow actor. Many contemporary poets contributed eulogies to Shakespeare; one of the best-known of these poems is by Ben Jonson, a fellow actor and, later, a friendly rival. Jonson also criticized Shakespeare's dramatic work in *Timber: or, Discoveries* (1641).

Certainly there are many things about Shakespeare's genius and career that the most diligent scholars do not know and cannot explain, but the facts that do exist are sufficient to establish Shakespeare's identity as a man and his authorship of the thirty-seven plays that reputable critics acknowledge to be his.

INTRODUCTION TO THE PLAY

Introduction

Shakespeare's *Macbeth* remains one of his most popular plays, both for classroom study and performance, and with good reason. Here we have the playwright's shortest play, but arguably his most intense, in terms both of its action and its portrayal of human relationships. The "butcher and his fiend-like queen" are among the most attractive villains in stage history, and the profound psychology with which Shakespeare imbues them is deliciously pleasurable for theater audience and student alike.

Historical Background

Macbeth was a real king of eleventh-century Scotland, whose history Shakespeare had read in several sources, principally the *Chronicles* of Holinshed, to which he referred for many of his other historical dramas. In Holinshed's account, Banquo and Macbeth combine to kill King Duncan after winning his favor in a battle against the Danes. The original story is full of wonderful details that show the cunning of the Scots and Macbeth, who slaughtered an entire Danish army not by brute force, but by cunning: first mixing a sleeping potion and sending it, like the Trojan horse, as a gift to the enemy army. Once they were asleep, Macbeth was able to kill them easily. Presumably from this incident, Shakespeare derived his idea of having Lady Macbeth administer a sleeping potion to the guards of King Duncan's chamber.

In Holinshed's account, however, although we learn that Macbeth's wife is ambitious to become queen, Lady Macbeth does not feature as an accomplice. Instead, Banquo joins forces with Macbeth in killing Duncan. As we shall see later, this particular confederacy of murderers presented Shakespeare with a problem.

Holinshed did not simply provide Shakespeare with a good story; *Macbeth* contains many examples of imagery and language that Shakespeare borrowed directly from his source, a practice common to all writers. For example, compare these words of Holinshed with Shakespeare's words.

Holinshed	*Shakespeare*
"What manner of women (saith he) are you, that seeme so little favourable unto me, whereas to my fellow heere, besides high offices, ye assign also the kingdom?" Banquho	"My noble partner / You greet with present grace, and great prediction / Of noble having, and of royal hope . . . to me you speak not." Banquo
Makbeth is afraid "lest he should be served of the same cup, as he had ministered to his predecessor."	Macbeth knows that, all too often, " . . . even-handed Justice / Commends th'ingredience of our poison'd chalice /To our own lips"

There are many more such examples. What does Shakespeare *add*, then? Primarily, the dialogue form of a play allows Shakespeare to examine the emotional relationships *between* characters with much greater realism. An audience going to Shakespeare's play would see ambition, accusation, fear, grief, courage, anger, and madness at first hand instead of via a narrator.

Secondly, as in his other plays, Shakespeare's genius lies in the human treatment that each character receives. The audience is made to feel that this awful tragedy could actually happen precisely because the characters are so three-dimensional. Lady Macbeth cannot sustain her mask of cruelty; Macbeth is racked with a tormented conscience. Banquo, in Shakespeare's version a good man, is nevertheless ambitious, too.

Thirdly, drama allows events to be linked and patterned in ironic ways. The idea of sleeplessness, for example, the punishment of a guilty mind, is shown literally in Act V, when Lady Macbeth sleepwalks and confesses her involvement with the murder of Duncan.

Finally, Shakespeare's mastery of the *soliloquy,* or solo speech, gives the audience the opportunity to see inside a character's mind, to witness, with some psychological accuracy, the intentions, hopes, and fears of these historical characters, something that a chronicler of history cannot do.

The Stage History of the Play

One of Shakespeare's main interests in writing *Macbeth* was to examine the nature of kingship, as he had already done in *Hamlet* and *King Lear*, written only a few years previously. In order to understand why he was so interested in this topic, we must examine briefly the fascinating early stage history of this play.

Probably written in 1605–1606, *Macbeth* was first performed for King James I of England less than a year after the infamous Gunpowder plot in which a group of Catholics attempted to blow up the king and the English parliament. A play that concerned treachery and regicide—the killing of a king—was bound to be topical and politically significant. There can be no real question of Shakespeare's wish to flatter a king whose interest in both the supernatural and the nature of kingship are all referred to so strongly in this play. Moreover, James I was descended from Scottish ancestors, the Stuarts, so a play concerning the early kings of Scotland was bound to appeal to him. Shakespeare's only problem was that the Stuarts were descended from Banquo who, as Holinshed's *Chronicle* makes clear, helped Macbeth murder the king. This explains why, in Shakespeare's play, Banquo cannot be the accomplice, a role that instead passes to Macbeth's wife.

So fascinated was James I in the notion of what makes a good king that he himself had written (in 1599) a handbook on good government, the *Basilikon Doron*. Some of these ideas of good kingship are listed by Malcolm as "the king-becoming graces" in Act IV, Scene 3 of *Macbeth*: "Justice, Verity, Temp'rance, Stableness, Bounty, Perseverance, Mercy, Lowliness, Devotion, Patience, Courage, Fortitude." Macbeth lacks all these kingly virtues, but his greatest vice is his impulse to lie—even to his own conscience—in his pursuit of power.

Macbeth and His Audience

Like all tragic heroes before him, Macbeth's greatest lie is to himself. He becomes blinded to his own ambition. His overbearing pride (or *hubris*) is so great that he fails to see as he stumbles toward his destiny. Perhaps only when Lady Macbeth commits her off-stage suicide does he begin to acknowledge the truth. "She should have died hereafter," he comments, and then adds "Tomorrow and tomorrow and tomorrow / Creeps in this petty pace from day to day / To the last syllable of recorded time. . . ."

These lines apply to us, not just as readers and playgoers, but as humans. We may not have committed murder, we may not have ambitions for power, but we all know how it feels to watch time passing. At this point in the play, we see a man emotionally raw, stripped momentarily of all his power, admitting—with self-awareness and, perhaps, with bitter self-irony—his share in the common human experience. This moment is only one of the few moments in the play when Macbeth does so. Immediately afterwards, he strides into battle with all his former arrogance, to his tragic end. Without these lines, we could not, perhaps, feel the tragedy in the same way.

We may not *be* Macbeth, but as playgoers and readers, we encounter what he does: We, too, experience visions of the supernatural. We, too, ask "Is it a dagger?" "Is it a ghost?" "Are they real?" The answer to all these questions is equivocal; they are real, in a way, and in another way, they are false, only tricks "paltering with us in a double sense." Even Macbeth is and is not real. He's an actor playing an actor, deeply aware of his twofold existence.

The play is peppered with references to the world of the theater, from the very beginning when we are seduced into a magic ritual by three characters who chant and dance around *their* stage. The banquet in Act III is a magnificent piece of staging, in which the director (Macbeth) is not allowed to direct as he wishes. Even the murder is an act, as distinct from the thought or intention of an act, as Lady Macbeth reminds her husband "Art thou afeard / To be the same in thine own act and valour / As thou art in desire?"

And so when we look at this man, we see an actor, directed by Fate, his wife, and himself, capable yet incapable, suffering from stage fright, yet knowing that he must go on if the play is to succeed. Looked at in this way, we begin to sympathize with Macbeth, and we suddenly recognize what is the truly great achievement of this play.

As in all good theatre, we're put on the spot just as Macbeth is: "*If* it were done . . .," but *will* it be done? If it *is* done, what will be its effect? And what would *we* do? At the same time, while we recognize that Macbeth *should* not act in the way he does, we must, nevertheless, ask ourselves why his acts in that way. The answers are far from simple.

Shakespeare's Language, Imagery, and Technique

English of this period can be quite difficult to understand at first, but remember that one reason for Shakespeare's popularity is that much of his language is actually very bold and clear. For instance, Macbeth famously says that there is sufficient blood on his hands to make the "green" of the ocean "red." Later, he uses the same metaphor, remarking that he must "wade" through an ocean of blood.

The trouble with *Macbeth* is that, as a psychological drama, the characters in the play (accidentally or on purpose) do *not* see things so clearly: This play is full of shadows, foreshadowings, and shadowy meanings. So Shakespeare has to inform his audience, while allowing the characters to remain mystified, or "in the dark." This is one reason why the play is full of questions, most famously "Is this a dagger?" The answer, for both Macbeth and the audience, is unclear.

Most scholars agree that one of the most effective ways in which Shakespeare's writing communicates is through the combination (or clusters) of images: In this play, images of strength and weakness, as well as ability and inability, are played off one another constantly. A good example is the image of the "milk of human kindness" which resurfaces later in Lady Macbeth's assertion that she would have murdered her own child while breast-feeding it—a contrast to Macbeth's weakness. The color of milk, white, is also used by both Macbeth and his wife, as an image of cowardice, while red—the color of blood—represents not only courage and the energy of life but also terror and the curtailment of life.

Another image contrast that is used repeatedly throughout the play is that of sleep and sleeplessness. Not only is Duncan murdered while he sleeps, but also Macbeth, Banquo, and Lady Macbeth have their rest disturbed by dreams. When Macbeth remarks "Duncan is in his grave; after life's fitful fever he sleeps well" (Act III, Scene 2), he is recalling the words with which his conscience (or Fate) spoke to him immediately after the murder: "Glamis hath murder'd sleep, and therefore Cawdor / Shall sleep no more, Macbeth shall sleep no more!" (II:2,41–42)

A Brief Synopsis

Set in medieval Scotland and partly based on a true historical account, *Macbeth* charts the bloody rise to power and tragic downfall of the warrior Macbeth. Already a successful soldier in the army of King Duncan, Macbeth is informed by Three Witches that he is to become king. As part of the same prophecy, the Witches predict that future Scottish kings will be descended not from Macbeth but from his fellow army captain, Banquo. Although initially prepared to wait for Fate to take its course, Macbeth is stung by ambition and confusion when King Duncan nominates his son Malcolm as his heir.

Returning to his castle, Macbeth allows himself to be persuaded and directed by his ambitious wife, who realizes that regicide—the murder of the king—is the quickest way to achieve the destiny that her husband has been promised. A perfect opportunity presents itself when King Duncan pays a royal visit to Macbeth's castle. At first Macbeth is loth to commit a crime that he knows will invite judgment, if not on earth then in heaven. Once more, however, his wife prevails upon him. Following an evening of revelry, Lady Macbeth drugs the guards of the king's bedchamber; then, at a given signal, Macbeth, although filled with misgivings, ascends to the king's room and murders him while he sleeps. Haunted by what he has done, Macbeth is once more reprimanded by his wife, whose inner strength seems only to have been increased by the treacherous killing. Suddenly, both are alarmed by a loud knocking at the castle door.

When the drunken porter of Macbeth's castle finally responds to the noise, he opens the door to Macduff, a loyal follower of the king, who has been asked to awake Duncan in preparation for the return journey. Macbeth indicates the location of the king's room, and Macduff discovers the body. When the murder is revealed, Macbeth swiftly kills the prime witnesses, the sleepy guards of the king's bedchamber, and Lady Macbeth faints. The assembled lords of Scotland, including Macbeth, swear to avenge the murder. With suspicion heavy in the air, the king's two sons flee the country: Donalbain to Ireland and Malcolm to raise an army in England.

Macbeth is duly proclaimed the new king of Scotland, but recalling the Witches' second prophecy, he arranges the murder of his fellow soldier Banquo and his son Fleance, both of whom represent a threat to his kingship according to the Witches' prophecy. The hired murderers kill Banquo but mistakenly allow Fleance to escape. At a celebratory banquet that night, Macbeth is thrown into a state of horror when the ghost of the murdered Banquo appears at the dining table. Again, his wife tries to strengthen Macbeth, but the strain is clearly beginning to show.

The following day, Macbeth returns to the same Witches who initially foretold his destiny. This time, the Witches not only confirm that the sons of Banquo will rule in Scotland, but they also add a new prophecy: Macbeth will be invincible in battle until the time when the forest of Birnam moves towards his stronghold at Dunsinane and until he meets an enemy "not born of woman." Dismissing both of these predictions as nonsense, Macbeth prepares for invasion.

When he is told that Macduff has deserted him, Macbeth begins the final stage of his tragic descent. His first move is the destruction of Macduff's wife and children. In England, Macduff receives the news at the very moment that he swears his allegiance to the young Malcolm. Malcolm persuades him that the murder of his family should act as the spur to revenge.

Meanwhile, in Scotland, Lady Macbeth has been taken ill: She walks in her sleep and seems to recall, in fragmentary memories, the details of the murder. Now, in a series of alternating scenes, the action of the play moves rapidly between the advancing army of Malcolm and the defensive preparations of Macbeth. When Malcolm's army disguise themselves with sawn-off branches, Macbeth sees what appears to be a wood moving towards his stronghold at Dunsinane. And when he finally meets Macduff in single combat, his sworn enemy reveals that he came into the world by cesarean section; he was not, precisely speaking, "born of woman." On hearing this news, Macbeth rejects one final time the Witches' prophecy. With a loud cry, he launches himself at Macduff and is slain. In the final scene, Malcolm is crowned as the new king of Scotland, to the acclaim of all.

List of Characters

Macbeth A captain in Duncan's army, later the Thane (Lord) of Glamis and Cawdor. When Three Witches predict that he will one day be king of Scotland, he takes his fate into his own hands, allowing his ambition and that of his wife to overcome his better judgement. His bloody reign culminates in a battle against Malcolm and the English forces.

Lady Macbeth The devilish wife of Macbeth, whose ambition helps to drive her husband toward the desperate act of murder. Subsequently, her husband's cruelty and her own guilt recoil on her, sending her into a madness from which she never recovers.

Banquo A fellow-captain and companion of Macbeth, who also receives a prophecy from the Witches: that his children will one day succeed to the throne of Scotland. This information is sufficient to spell his death at the hands of the resentful Macbeth, who is later haunted by Banquo's ghost.

Duncan King of Scotland. His victories against rebellious kinsmen and the Norwegians have made him a popular and honored king. His decision to pass the kingdom to his son Malcolm provokes his untimely death at the hands of Macbeth.

Fleance Banquo's son, who, by escaping Macbeth's plot on his life, will go on to be father to a line of kings.

Donalbain and Malcolm Duncan's two sons. Fearful of implication in their father's murder, they flee Scotland, Donalbain to Ireland and Malcolm to England, where he raises a large army with the intention of toppling the tyrant Macbeth.

Macduff A thane (nobleman) of Scotland who discovers the murdered King Duncan. Suspecting Macbeth and eventually turning against him, Macduff later flees to England to join Malcolm. When Macbeth arranges the murder of his wife and children, Macduff swears personal revenge.

Lennox, Ross, Menteth, Angus, Caithness Thanes of Scotland, all of whom eventually turn against the tyrannical Macbeth.

The Porter, the Old Man, the Doctors Three commentators on events, all of whom have a certain degree of wisdom and foresight. The Porter hints at the Hell-like nature of Macbeth's castle; the Old Man associates the murder of King Duncan with the instability of the natural world; the Doctors recognize disease and disorder even though they cannot cure it.

The Witches Three agents of Fate who reveal the truth (or part of it) to Macbeth and Banquo and who later appear to confirm the downfall and tragic destiny of the tyrannical Macbeth.

Character Map

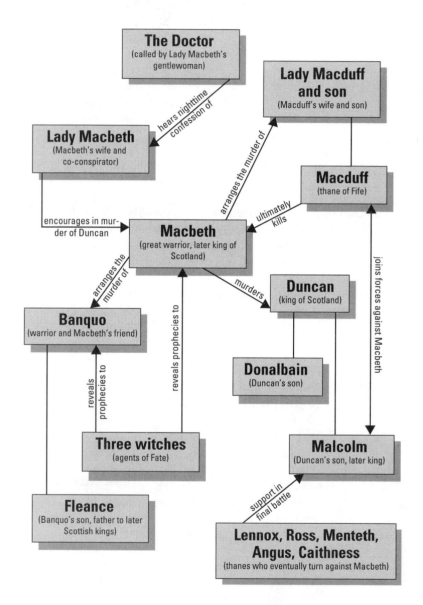

The Doctor (called by Lady Macbeth's gentlewoman)

hears nighttime confession of

Lady Macbeth (Macbeth's wife and co-conspirator)

Lady Macduff and son (Macduff's wife and son)

arranges the murder of

Macduff (thane of Fife)

ultimately kills

encourages in murder of Duncan

Macbeth (great warrior, later king of Scotland)

arranges the murder of

reveals prophecies to

murders

joins forces against Macbeth

Banquo (warrior and Macbeth's friend)

Duncan (king of Scotland)

reveals prophecies to

Donalbain (Duncan's son)

Three witches (agents of Fate)

Malcolm (Duncan's son, later king)

Fleance (Banquo's son, father to later Scottish kings)

support in final battle

Lennox, Ross, Menteth, Angus, Caithness (thanes who eventually turn against Macbeth)

CRITICAL COMMENTARIES

Act I—Scene 1

Summary

In a desolate place blasted by thunderstorms, Three Witches meet to predict the future.

Commentary

Macbeth begins in "an open place"—a place without any landmarks or buildings—with the appearance of the three "weird sisters," as they later call themselves. The Old English word "wyrd," or "weird" means "Fate," which is exactly the origin of these Witches: They are the Fates of classical mythology, one of whom spun the thread of a person's life, one of whom measured it, and one of whom cut it. The bleakness of the scene is a dramatic representation both of the wild Scottish landscape in which the play is set and the more universal wilderness of man's existence.

The Three Witches' speech is written in short rhyming verse that imitates the casting of a spell. The women's language is also full of the imagery of witchcraft and of chaotic weather: thunder, lightning, rain, fog, and "filthy air." The lines "When the battle's lost and won" and "Fair is foul and foul is fair" are the most significant in the scene. On the one hand, these contradictory statements are the kind of riddles we would expect from witches; on the other, the lines suggest a paradox that runs throughout the play: Life frequently presents a confused picture of events in which discerning truth from falsehood is difficult.

Glossary

(Here and in the following glossary sections, difficult words and phrases, as well as allusions and historical references, are explained.)

Graymalkin, Paddock (8) grey cat, toad; both "familiars" or witches' assistants

Act I—Scene 2

Summary

Scotland is at war. King Duncan faces not only his own rebellious kinsmen but also an invasion by King Sweno of the Norwegians. In this scene, Duncan receives three significant reports: the death of the rebel Macdonald at the hands of "brave Macbeth"; Macbeth's action against the Norwegians; and the treachery of the Thane of Cawdor, who has sided with the enemy. In each case, Macbeth's heroism shines out, leading to victory for Scotland and surrender by Sweno. Finally, Duncan orders Cawdor's execution and arranges for his title to pass to Macbeth.

Commentary

Literary Device

A captain of Duncan's army makes the initial report of the battle. At first, he says, the outcome of the fighting was in doubt. To describe the inertia of the two armies, the captain uses a metaphor of two drowning men, who gain no advantage by clinging together but instead "choke their art." At this stage in the battle, it had appeared that Fortune, like a "smiling . . . whore"—a traditional personification of her fickleness—would support Macdonald. It was left to the brave warrior Macbeth, "disdaining Fortune," to reverse this situation.

The introduction of Macbeth as a warrior hero is crucial to the play, for tragedy depends on our witnessing the downfall of an already great man. Phrases such as "Valour's minion" (the servant of Courage) and "Bellona's bridegroom" (the husband of War) exemplify Macbeth's superheroism. His strength is underscored by the captain's graphic account of Macbeth's actions on the battlefield. Macbeth did not simply kill Macdonald; he "unseam'd him from the nave to the chops, / And fix'd his head upon our battlements" (22–23)—a reference that foreshadows Macbeth's death at the end of the play.

Macbeth's reputation on the battlefield is further enhanced by the similes of the Captain's second report, in which Macbeth and his fellow-captain, Banquo, are compared to "eagles" and "lions" unafraid of the timid Norwegians, who themselves are likened to "sparrows" or "a hare." Symbolically, the lion appears on the royal coat of arms of the kings of Scotland. Macbeth's and Banquo's fighting is compared to the action of artillery pieces (even though, historically, this battle would have been a sword fight). Finally, Macbeth is credited with nothing less than recreating "Golgotha," the scene of Christ's crucifixion.

The Thane of Ross enters the scene with a third report: Once more, the result of the battle is doubtful, and once more both combatants are seen on equal terms—"self-comparisons"—until the outcome is decided in Scotland's favor by Macbeth. The scene ends with two resolutions: First, the Norwegians "crave composition"; that is, they beg for a truce. Second, and more importantly for the story, the disloyal Thane of Cawdor is condemned to execution and his title granted to Macbeth. The language in Scene 2 captures much of the activity, urgency, and gruesome realism of battle. Lines such as "the Norweyan banners flout the sky / And fan our people cold" give a cinematic feel to the scene and remind us that the play concerns a wider world and that its moral questions, when they come, do so as well.

Scene 2 establishes the opposing idea of order and the related theme of orderly or honorable behavior. Duncan himself is established as a figurehead of order who honors the valor of the bleeding captain and, in two grand rhyming couplets at the end of the scene, pronounces his favor of Macbeth.

Glossary

kerns, Gallowglasses (13) light infantry, heavy infantry.

gins his reflection (25) starts to turn in its seasonal course.

Bellona's bridegroom (55) bridegroom to the goddess of war (i.e. Macbeth).

lapp'd in proof (55) covered in armor.

Act I–Scene 3

Summary

With a clap of thunder, the Witches reappear. Having demonstrated their power by casting a terrible curse upon a sailor whose wife offended one of them, they encounter Macbeth and Banquo as the two soldiers ride from the battlefield. The sisters make three prophecies, the first two regarding Macbeth and the last regarding Banquo. Macbeth shall be named as Thane of Cawdor and then king; Banquo, although he shall not himself rule in Scotland, will be father to future generations of kings. Immediately, the Witches vanish into thin air, leaving the two captains in amazement. Ross and Angus arrive on the scene to confirm what we already know, that Macbeth is to be invested with the thaneship of Cawdor. The Witches' first prophecy has come true.

Commentary

Literary Device

The opening of Scene 3 does more than to simply recall us to the world of the supernatural of Act I, Scene 1: The Witches' curse of the sailor foreshadows what Fate has in store for Macbeth. The sailor is the captain of a ship, in the same way that Macbeth is to become "captain" of his land; like the sailor, Macbeth will be blown by the tempests of ill Fortune. Sleep will be denied to both. Famously, Macbeth later believes that, in murdering Duncan, he "has murder'd sleep," and both he and Lady Macbeth are denied "Sleep that knits up the ravelled sleeve of care." Finally, the metaphor of a storm at sea is traditionally used to refer to confusion and the unpredictability of events.

Macbeth's first words ("So foul and fair a day I have not seen") ironically recall the Witches' "foul is fair" in Scene 1, but Banquo is the first to spot the weird sisters, remarking on the Witches' ambiguous and confused appearance: They "look not like the inhabitants of the earth, / And yet are on it"; they seem to understand him, and yet he cannot be sure; they "should be women," and yet they are bearded. Later in the scene, Macbeth remarks that the Witches "seem'd corporal [physical]" and yet they vanish like bubbles "into the air."

No such ambiguity occurs in the response of the Witches to Macbeth: He is Thane of Glamis, he is Thane of Cawdor, and he shall be King. This contrast between what is uncertain and what is certain, or between what is confused and what is ordered or ordained by Fate, is one of the crucial structural components in the writing of this play, and it is clear that Shakespeare wants us to see it.

Banquo's reaction to this peculiar prophecy is understandable rather than an example of professional rivalry. He has been linked in name with Macbeth and, so far, enjoys equal merit with his friend. Why should he not also have his future predicted? But the Witches' answer to him is more riddling: "lesser . . . and greater," "not so happy . . . much happier," "get kings . . . be none" all suggest a more unpredictable future.

Noteworthy in this scene is the way in which Shakespeare registers the psychological response of both Macbeth and Banquo. The questions "Whither . . . ?", "Were . . . ?", "Have we . . . ?" and so on paint a picture of shared incomprehension. Shakespeare cleverly combines Macbeth's and Banquo's confusion at the Witches' vanishing with their disbelief at what has been spoken. The reference to "the insane root that takes the reason prisoner" suggests the working of a powerful drug, and the clear impression is that they feel they have been dreaming.

Ross arrives and announces that Macbeth is to be the new Thane of Cawdor, thus confirming the first prophecy of the Witches. Banquo and Macbeth are struck dumb for the second time, but now Shakespeare contrasts their responses. Banquo is aware of the possibility that the prophecies may have been the work of supernatural dark forces, as exemplified in his lines "What? Can the Devil speak true?" (108) and "oftentimes, to win us to our harm, / The instruments of Darkness tell us truths . . . —(only) to betray us" (123–125). Macbeth is more ambiguous. His speech is full of what will now become his trademark—questioning, doubting, weighing up, and seeking to justify: "This supernatural soliciting / Cannot be ill; cannot be good" (130–131).

Nevertheless, however much he reasons, Macbeth cannot reconcile the fact of the truth of the first prophecy with his intense and unnatural fear, or what he calls his "horrible imaginings." He admits to being so shaken by the news that he feels that his reason has been taken over by his imagination. The line "Nothing is, but what is not" is ambiguous. The expression could indicate confusion between the world we think of as real and the world of dreams, a neat summary of a confused mind. But how confused *is* Macbeth at this point? If he is capable of arguing that the prophecies are neither evil nor good, he is capable of accepting that nothing that exists has any existence or meaning. This interpretation could open Macbeth to dangerous and unjustifiable deeds. If he can make himself believe that "Nothing is, but what is not," then Macbeth's respect for order, for hierarchy, for the King, is also nullified. He can, literally, get away with murder.

Glossary

mounch'd (4) munched

aroynt! (6) begone!

runyon (6) hag

card (16) a sea-chart

penthouse lid (20) eyelid.

bark (24) boat

Sinel (71) Macbeth's father.

corporal (81) bodily, physical

line the rebel . . . vantage (112) secretly give aid to the rebels.

trifles (125) trivial gifts

swelling act . . . theme (128) the developing royal drama

cleave (146) fit

pains (151) service to me

interim (155) meanwhile

Act I—Scene 4

Summary

In the palace court room, King Duncan receives the news of the execution of Cawdor and delivers formal thanks to Macbeth and Banquo for their part in the battle. Then, to the private astonishment of Macbeth, Duncan announces that his successor as king, whenever that may be, will be his son Malcolm.

Commentary

The dramatic function of this short scene is twofold. First, it gives an opportunity to observe the relationship between Macbeth and Duncan; second, it provides Macbeth with further fuel for his ambitious claim on the kingdom.

Literary Device

Malcolm's report of the execution of the disloyal Thane of Cawdor emphasizes the dignity with which even a traitor can go to his death, but Duncan's reply is even more ironic. "There's no art to find the mind's construction in the face" has a proverbial flavor to it—never judge a book by its cover—but it's also a sad admission that even Duncan was unable to predict the treachery of Cawdor. Such is the human side of kingship. Exactly at the moment that Duncan speaks the line, Shakespeare seals the irony by having Macbeth enter the court room.

Literary Device

Formal speeches are exchanged, both Macbeth and Banquo giving humble and loyal replies to their king. The imagery at this point in the scene largely refers to growth and fertility. The king clearly sees Macbeth as a potential successor: "I have begun to plant thee, and will labour / To make thee full of growing" (28–29). The metaphor is continued by Banquo, who promises the king that, if he too is allowed to grow in the king's favor, he will dedicate "the harvest" to Duncan. At this point, the scene recalls Banquo's earlier line when he asked the Witches if they could "look into the seeds of time / And say which one will grow, and which will not" (I:3,58–59). The irony of giving the earlier "seeds" line and now the "harvest" line to Banquo is that these expressions symbolize the seed, or children, of Banquo himself, who are to inherit the kingdom, according to the Witches' third prophecy.

Note the way in which Shakespeare plays with images such as these. Often he builds up a cluster of related images (as here, "plant," "growing," "grow," and "harvest") precisely in order to establish a sense of irony. In the next speeches, for example, the king first invests all those who deserve his thanks with "signs of nobleness, like stars." Only a few lines later, Macbeth, frustrated and angry at the news of Malcolm's investiture as Prince of Cumberland, breathes to himself the words "Stars! Hide your fires! Let not light see my black and deep desires" (50–51).

Here, the juxtaposition of images of starlight and the cancellation of starlight emphasizes the great opposition between the king and Macbeth and between good and evil, an opposition that is ironically reinforced by the king's final lines to Banquo, once more praising Macbeth. The phrase "peerless kinsman" gives added poignancy: The historical Macbeth was the cousin of Duncan, and his crime will not simply be regicide, but the willful destruction of the head of a family.

Glossary

became him (8) suited him

construction (12) intention

which is not us'd for you (44) which you are not used to

harbinger (45) forerunner

Act I—Scene 5

Summary

At Macbeth's home, the castle of Inverness, Lady Macbeth reads a letter from her husband concerning his meeting with the Witches. She is immediately aware of the significance of their prophetic words and, on being informed that King Duncan will be paying a royal visit to Inverness, makes up her mind to carry out the murder of the king in order to hasten the prophecy. In doing so, she suggests that her husband is weak—he contains too much of "the milk of human kindness." When Macbeth arrives from the court of Duncan, bearing news of the king's forthcoming visit, his wife makes her plans clear to him.

Commentary

The letter, read alone on stage by Lady Macbeth, reiterates the Witches' prophecy of Act I. Significantly, in his letter, Macbeth says nothing of their prophecy to Banquo; perhaps he is already afraid of its implications. Equally significantly, he sets up Lady Macbeth as his "dearest partner of greatness." She will indeed become his partner in crime, but much more than that: Apart from the fatal blow itself, she will be responsible for controlling Macbeth's passions and—to an extent—his actions.

Immediately after she finishes the letter, Lady Macbeth's mind goes to work. Her words "shalt be" uncannily reflect those of the Witches' prophecy. At this point, Lady Macbeth herself has virtually become an agent of Fate, just like the Weird Sisters. But immediately her thoughts turn to possible failings in her husband. He is "too full of the milk of human kindness" to commit murder; he *would* be great, he *would* have a high position, he *would* wrongly win that position, but in each case, some other aspect of his character *would not*. In this case, she says, there is only one solution. She must "pour [her] spirits in thine ear." Any member of Shakespeare's audience who had seen his play *Hamlet* four years previously would be more than aware of the significance of this line, for in that play the good King Claudius is murdered by poison administered through the ear. The scene is rapidly becoming darker.

Lady Macbeth is one of the most powerful female characters in literature. The fact that we meet her alone on stage means that we are privy to her innermost thoughts, which are filled with the imagery of death and destruction. And when she speaks, in her next soliloquy, of her "fell purpose," her intentions are described in the most grotesque and frightening terms. First she bids the spirits to literally deprive her of her femininity, to thicken her blood, and to stop her ability to weep. Next, she prays that those same evil spirits should suckle her, converting what should be her nourishing mother's milk to "gall" (bitterness). Lastly, she calls upon the night itself to hide her actions in a "blanket" of darkness. It is no coincidence that these last words reflect those of Macbeth in the previous scene: Shakespeare is creating a strong verbal bond between husband and wife that will continue throughout the play.

When Macbeth enters his castle, his wife greets him in a way that again recalls the words of the Witches; in particular the words "all-hail" and "hereafter" chill the audience, for they are the exact words spoken to Macbeth by the Witches. The dialogue that follows their initial encounter is fast, urgent, and disturbing. Shakespeare uses half-line breaks to intensify the drama of the moment, each "partner in crime" picking up the rhythm of the other's speech:

M: My dearest love,
    Duncan comes here tonight.

LM: And when goes hence?

M: Tomorrow, as he purposes.

LM: Oh, never
    Shall sun that morrow see!

Shakespeare uses the same technique immediately after the murder.

In the lines that follow, Lady Macbeth uses several significant metaphors of concealment: Macbeth's face is like "a book, where men / May read strange matters" (63–64); then, in a brilliantly ironic reference to the Genesis story, "Look like the innocent flower, / But be the serpent under it" (66–67). The apparent paradise promised by the Witches is soon to become a hell. An important psychological point is also made: Lady Macbeth herself does not hide her feelings in the same way that Macbeth does. She is not rapt in wonderment, simply practical. The last line of the scene, "Leave all the rest to me," is quite modern in its tone. With this blunt and chilling imperative, Lady Macbeth completes her transformation from woman to man. From now on, she plays on the reversal of roles; she has adopted the role of "man of action," forcing her husband into the more passive role of accomplice.

Glossary

lose the dues (12) miss the reward

hie thee hither (25) come here quickly

chastise (27) beat off, chase away

golden round (28) the crown (kingship)

metaphysical (29) supernatural

effect and it (47) the result and the plan

favour (72) complexion

Act I—Scene 6

Summary

King Duncan and his retinue arrive at Inverness. Various formal greetings are exchanged between the king and Lady Macbeth, who, like a chameleon, now takes on the more typical role of perfect hostess.

Commentary

Duncan's speech on his arrival at Inverness is heavy with dramatic irony: Not only is the "seat" (the surroundings) of the castle "pleasant," but even the air is sweeter than that to which the king is accustomed. The presence of the martlet (a summer bird) serves to heighten the irony. As far as the king is concerned, the castle, from the outside at least, appears to be a paradise. Contrast this picture of delight with the imagery of hell that forms the substance of the Porter scene (Act II, Scene 3).

The king's address to Lady Macbeth and her subsequent reply are full of the heightened language of formal introduction: "God @'ild you," "We rest your hermits (your servants) ever." Of course, her elaborate greeting contrasts her language of the previous scene and emphasizes her falsity.

The stage directions that frame this scene are full of the pomp and ceremony of a royal visit. To a musical accompaniment, food and drink are transported from one side of the stage to the other. Although the audience does not see the revelry on stage, Shakespeare intends us to understand that the king is to be well entertained.

Glossary

temple-haunting martlet (4) bird that nests in church porches

loved mansionry (5) favorite building

jutty . . . vantage (6) eaves, convenient corner

pendent (7) hanging

procreant cradle (7) nest

haunt (8) regularly visit

love . . . love (11) As king, I must always acknowledge my subjects' love even though doing so is a burden to me. But I must tell you that in taking trouble for me, you win God's thanks.

All . . . house (14) Even if I were to double my efforts on your behalf, it would be nothing compared with the honour you pay by visiting our house.

cours'd (21) chased

purpose . . . purveyor (21) intended to arrive before him

holp (23) helped

in compt . . . audit (26) on your account, to be assessed by you

Act I—Scene 7

Summary

Alone, Macbeth ponders the deed that he is about to perform. He is aware of the powerful reasons for murdering the king, but is nagged by self-doubt arising from his fear of retribution both in heaven and on earth and by his likely loss of reputation. However, any such fears are dismissed by his wife in the same practical tone that she used in Act I. Her taunting of her husband's weakness, coupled with the efficiency of her own plan, convince Macbeth that he should take on the "horrid deed."

Commentary

Style & Language

The imagery of Macbeth's soliloquy reveals the intentions he would like to achieve ("assassination," "success"), but its construction shows the workings of a mind still very much in confusion. Notice the insistent repetition of individual words—*if, were, done, be, but,* and *here*—each repeated two or three times within the first few lines. Within the fluid construction of this soliloquy, words and sounds constantly attract and suggest each other, giving the impression of a train of thought. All this begs the question of whether Macbeth, able to rationalize and express his thoughts, is thereby revealed as an intelligent, poetic soul. And if that's the case, does he appear more human, more or less capable of sinning, and, worrysome for the audience, more or less capable of winning their sympathy?

It is the thought of something after death that puzzles Macbeth. Throughout the speech, his words recall those of Shakespeare's earlier tragic hero, Hamlet. In paraphrase, Macbeth wonders whether the act of murder itself must, by necessity, carry consequences in "the life to come" or whether judgment will await him in this life. Macbeth is simultaneously aware of the duplicity and imbalance of the proposed murder (he is Duncan's relative, subject, and host, yet he is to be his killer) and of the equality and balance of earthly and heavenly law: "this even-handed Justice / Commends the ingredients of our poison'd chalice / To our own lips" (11–12).

Of further concern to Macbeth is the disparity between his own reputation and the world's perception of Duncan as a good and virtuous king. The final section of the speech contains an apocalyptic vision in which he imagines Duncan's virtue and pity proclaimed as if by angels and cherubim from a storm-filled sky. This doom-laden vision, whose imagery (for example, "trumpet-tongued") reflects that of the biblical Day of Judgment, gives way in turn to a nagging self-doubt. Whereas he pictures the angels and cherubim "horsed upon the sightless couriers of the air," Macbeth admits that he himself has "no spur / to prick the sides of my intent but only / Vaulting ambition which o'erleaps itself / And falls on the other [side]" (25–28).

Character Insight

Lady Macbeth must immediately detect Macbeth's self-doubt. When Macbeth admits to her that his golden reputation might lose its "gloss," she sets out to strengthen his resolve by mocking his perceived weakness. Her questions drive further the wedge between daring and doing, between courage and action, between desire and fulfillment. To these, she adds a distinction between masculinity and femininity: In contrast to her own self-proclaimed manliness, she pours scorn upon her husband's lack of courage. She tells him he is "green," "a coward," and that he resembles the proverbial "poor cat" who wanted the fish but would not get its paws wet. Finally, and most damningly, she tells him that her own lack of pity would extend to murdering her own child as it suckled at her breast. With this one terrifying example, she confirms that "the milk of human kindness" is absent in her.

Style & Language

The next paragraph commences with a shift in tone—no less pragmatic but even more ruthlessly efficient—as Lady Macbeth switches her attention to the details of the murder itself. Her plan to drug the guards with alcohol is couched in metaphorical language derived from the ancient science of alchemy. The words "receipt," "fume," and "limbeck" specifically refer to this process, whose purpose was to turn base metal (such as lead) into gold. It is heavily ironic that, in the Macbeths' experiment, that which is gold—the king himself—will become base and doubly ironic that Macbeth's golden reputation will be reduced to worthlessness.

Macbeth has been convinced. In words that uncannily recall his wife's, he now puts on the mantle of murderer: the monosyllabic "False face must hide what the false heart doth know" has a certainty to it that completely overturns his earlier vacillation.

Glossary

trammel up (3) obstruct, prevent

surcease (4) death

shoal (6) sandbank

faculties (17) kingly powers

taking-off (20) murder

sightless couriers (23) invisible winds

ornament of life (42) the crown

adage (44) proverb

fitness (53) appropriateness

sticking-place (61) its limit

wassail (65) entertainment

receipt . . . limbeck (68) container for an alchemist's solution; here, Macbeth's plan

mettle (74) courage

corporal agent (81) physical part of myself

Act II—Scene 1

Summary

As Macbeth makes his way toward the king's bedchamber, he encounters Banquo with his son Fleance. Banquo has been unable to sleep and explains to Macbeth that he has been dreaming of the weird sisters. After arranging to meet again in order to discuss the matter, Banquo asserts his allegiance to the king and bids good night to Macbeth. No sooner is Macbeth alone, than he has an extraordinary experience. Either in the heat of the moment or through some supernatural visitation, he sees a ghostly dagger indicating the way to the Duncan. Convinced that "there's no such thing," he climbs to the king's chamber.

Commentary

The opening dialogue sets the scene: It is past midnight, the moon has set, and the "candles" of heaven—the stars—cannot be seen. Symbolically, the airy lightness that greeted Duncan's arrival at the castle in Act I has completely vanished, to be replaced by brooding darkness.

Literary Device

In this opening scene of Act II, as in the later Porter scene, the audience feels momentarily suspended from the action but in no way removed from the intensity of emotion as the innocent Banquo and his son pass the time of night. The moment at which Banquo so very nearly draws his sword on a potential intruder (actually Macbeth) is a master-stroke of dramatic irony: Banquo has no idea of what the audience knows.

Style & Language

The dagger speech (32–65) is, deservedly, one of the most celebrated in Shakespeare. Like "If it were done" (Act I, Scene 7), this soliloquy is a fascinating piece of stage psychology. The structure of the lines precisely echoes the swings from lucidity to mental disturbance that characterize Macbeth throughout the play. There are three false alarms: "I see thee still . . . I see thee yet . . . I see thee still!" Between each of these alarms comes a moment of respite in which Macbeth appeals to the world of the physical senses: "Art thou not . . . sensible to feeling?" "Mine eyes are made the fools of the other senses," and "It is the bloody business which informs thus to mine eyes."

Style & Language

Nevertheless, as in the earlier scene with his wife, Macbeth eventually capitulates. The urge to become king is now strong in him. In his final lines, as he ascends to the king's chamber, he imagines himself as the personification of Murder itself, stealthily making its way towards its victim. The change of tone to one of high rhetoric and classical allusion (Hecate, Tarquin) may seem out of place, but not if we imagine Macbeth putting on a "mask" of language in preparation for the murder. The distinction between word and deed in the last line is an idea that occurs frequently in Shakespeare. What we say and what we do are frequently very different matters. But in the final couplet, Macbeth seems to transfer his own doubts concerning the afterlife to Duncan: Whether the king will go to heaven or hell is now an academic matter; ironically, for Macbeth himself, the outcome is likely to be more certain.

Glossary

husbandry in heaven (4) the gods are economical with their starlight

cleave to my consent (25) approve of my plan

augment (27) support

dudgeon (46) handle

gouts (46) drops

Hecate (52) goddess of witchcraft

Tarquin (46) murderous king of Rome

prate (58) prattle

Act II–Scene 2

Summary

Having drugged the guards of Duncan's chamber, Lady Macbeth now meets her husband in the lower courtyard as he emerges from the king's room itself. Macbeth's conscience is clearly disturbed by what he has done, and once more his wife criticizes his lack of firmness. The success of their plot is also in jeopardy because Macbeth has brought the daggers with him. Lady Macbeth returns to the scene of the murder in order to place the daggers and to smear the king's sleeping servants with blood, a deed that presents her with none of the horror that now affects Macbeth. As the scene closes, we hear, with the Macbeths, a loud and persistent knocking at the door.

Commentary

Literary Device

Lady Macbeth's opening words introduce a new level of emotional intensity. Fear of failure has been replaced with fear of discovery, and even though she describes herself as drunk with boldness and on fire with passion, she is just as easily alarmed as her husband is by the tiniest noises and movements. Her swift changes of thought and speech foreshadow the language of her final lapse into madness in the sleepwalking scene (Act V, Scene 1), when she relives these same moments.

Yet, despite all this, Lady Macbeth appears to be sufficiently hardened to the deed to be able to make several horribly ironic comments, including the observation that she would have committed the murder herself, had she not been put off the idea by the resemblance of the sleeping king to her own father. Note the similarity of this line—by which she seems to excuse something lacking in herself—with her earlier taunt to Macbeth that she would have dashed out the brains of her own child had she sworn to do so. The fact is that what Lady Macbeth *would do* her husband has *actually done*. The total reversal of roles that she anticipated cannot now occur because, despite his stricken conscience, Macbeth has done what she could never do.

Style & Language

The quick-fire dialogue and fragmented line structure in this part of the scene denote a sense of frightened urgency in both characters. Macbeth's concern centers on two major areas. First, he believes he has "murder'd sleep." Sleep, he argues, ought to bring physical calm in the same way that prayer soothes the spirit. But in his case, the ability both to pray and to sleep has been cancelled. Macbeth is haunted by the knowledge that he will never again rest easy in his own bed: "Glamis hath murdered sleep, and therefore Cawdor / Shall sleep no more, Macbeth shall sleep no more!" (41–42). Lady Macbeth, refusing to accept such "brainsickly" thoughts, reminds Macbeth of the familiar comparison that "the sleeping and the dead / Are but as pictures." Ironically, she is the one who will be kept from sleeping by the picture of death long after it has left Macbeth's mind.

The second area of Macbeth's concern is the bloodiness of the deed and specifically the fact that his own hands bear witness to the unnatural deed of murder. Again, for Lady Macbeth, blood is only like paint used to daub the picture of death and can be easily washed off. But Macbeth is aware of the deep stain beneath the surface. His capacity for recognizing the grand scale of his action, which foreshadows his later remark that he is "in blood stepped in so far," is missing in Lady Macbeth.

At this point, the knocking begins. Like the beating of the heart in Edgar Allan Poe's short story "The Tell-Tale Heart," the noise is partly the knocking of their consciences and partly an actual exterior knocking. Symbolically, the knocking is the knocking of justice, or of vengeance.

Glossary

bellman (3) man who summoned condemned prisoners

surfeited (5) drunk

their charge (6) that is, Duncan

second course (38) that is, at the banquet of life

gild (55) paint them with golden blood

incarnadine (61) make red

Act II—Scene 3

Summary

The knocking continues, but the porter does not immediately open the door. Instead, he plays a game with himself in which he imagines himself as the porter of hell and jokes about the kind of sinners he might let in. Eventually, however, he opens the door to Lennox and Macduff, who have been commanded to call upon the king to arrange the royal departure. It is early morning, and most of those in the castle are still asleep. One who is not is Macbeth, and he directs Macduff to the king's chamber. Only a moment passes before the news breaks: King Duncan has been murdered.

On hearing the terrible revelation, the Macbeths' acts are beyond suspicion, but Macbeth admits to having killed the guards of the King's chamber—not part of the original plan—and Lady Macbeth faints. The assembled thanes of Scotland resolve to avenge the act of treason. Duncan's sons, Malcolm and Donalbain, thinking themselves open to the charge of murdering their father, plan to flee to England and Ireland.

Commentary

Literary Device

This busy scene begins with a moment of light comedy, which serves to heighten the suspense. The porter of Macbeth's castle, drunk from the previous night's revels, complains that his job is worse than that of the porter of hell. In a private game with the audience, he engages in a piece of stand-up comedy in which he imagines himself as that beleaguered servant, opening and closing the gate on the damned. The first two examples he uses (that of a farmer and an equivocator) have specific religious and historical connotations. A few months before *Macbeth* was performed at court in front of the Protestant King James I, the infamous Gunpowder Plot (the aim of which was to murder the English king) took place. The conspirators, including Guy Fawkes, may have been encouraged by a Catholic convert called John Garnett, whose nickname was "farmer." The practice of lying in court about one's religion by employing confusing or ambiguous language was known as equivocation. Many examples of ambiguous language are heard throughout *Macbeth*, and of course the words of the Witches themselves are not entirely clear. So the porter's examples are not entirely without significance, even though they may be unintentional.

The humor continues when the porter unbolts the door to Macduff and Lennox and offers a series of bawdy jokes, momentarily distracting the audience from the fact that Macbeth must at this very moment be washing his hands of the blood of the previous scene. Then Macbeth enters, apparently at ease, to direct Macduff to the king's room.

Theme

While Macduff goes to wake the king, Lennox remarks upon the extraordinary weather of the previous night. His catalogue of unnatural events—high winds, screaming and wailing voices, the calling of birds, and tremors in the earth—is apocalyptic in character and suggests a direct connection between the events of the universe at large and the events within the castle. Macbeth's response—"'Twas a rough night"—is so anticlimactic as to provoke incredulity. Is Lennox's subsequent line—"My young remembrance cannot parallel / A fellow to it" (64-65)—intended to be spoken with puzzlement at Macbeth's reaction?

Style & Language

At this moment, the dam breaks. Note that the literal truth of Macduff's announcement—"Our royal master's murdered"—is preceded by several lines in which the murder is depicted in a figurative or metaphorical fashion, almost as if Macduff dare not name the deed: "Murther hath broke ope / The Lord's anointed Temple," "destroy your sight / With a new Gorgon," and "see / The great doom's image!" It's interesting to compare these lines of Macduff's, spoken in all innocence, with those of the all-too-guilty Macbeth, who also approaches the matter metaphorically: "The wine of life is drawn . . . and "The spring, the head, the fountain of your blood / Is stopp'd . . .."

Excusing his own outburst of passion in killing the guards of the king's chamber, Macbeth explains that he could not act otherwise when he saw the king: "Here lay Duncan, / His silver skin laced with his golden blood; / And his gashed stabs looked like a breach in nature / For ruin's wasteful entrance" (113–116). That Macbeth cannot refrain from the use of metaphor may be an indication that he, too, cannot bear to consider the bloody truth. His words are at once highly poetic and, at the same time, enormously revealing of the deep ironies of which Macbeth must be aware. Not only has he "murdered sleep," but he has destroyed the actual fabric of nature.

For whatever reason—perhaps because Lady Macbeth thinks that Macbeth's powerfully rhetorical speech is the precursor to an admission of their combined guilt—she suddenly faints. Certainly, as soon as she is carried from the stage, the pace changes. There is no more time for speculation: Macbeth and the other thanes rapidly swear to meet "in manly readiness" to avenge this act of "treasonous malice." Malcolm and Donalbain alone remain to voice their understandable concerns: Their semi-proverbial sentences "To show an unfelt sorrow is an office / Which the false man does easy" (138–139) and "Where we are / There's daggers in men's smiles" (141–142) both uncomfortably recall the language of earlier scenes.

Glossary

old (2) frequent

napkins (6) handkerchiefs

equivocator (9) liar

hose (14) trousers

made a shift to cast him (40) with effort I overpowered the drink

Gorgon (71) hideous monster than turns beholders to stone

lees (93) dregs

vault (94) wine cellar, *punning on* grave

pauser (109) restraining force of

auger-hole (120)   the tiniest crevice

scruples (127) doubts

undivulg'd pretence (129) undisclosed plot of treason

the near in blood . . . bloody (142) close relations are more likely to be suspected of murder

warrant in that theft (143) this kind of stealing (away) is justified

Act II—Scene 4

Summary

On his way from the castle, the Thane of Ross encounters an Old Man, who confirms the widespread reports of disruption in the natural world. Macduff appears with fresh news that Duncan is buried, that his sons have fled, and that the kingship has passed to Macbeth. The opening prophecies of the Witches have been completed.

Commentary

Like the Witches, the Old Man is a traditional figure in many works of literature. In contrast to the Witches' vision of what *will* be, the old man exemplifies the certainty of what *has* been: The notion of age, tradition and natural continuity, as well as wisdom are all bound up in this single figure. In words that recall those of the much younger Lennox in the previous scene, the old man describes how the world that he knows and trusts has been turned on its head. All the named events are not simply natural disasters; they are reversals of the expected natural order: Daylight has been replaced by night; a falcon (a bird of prey) has been killed by an owl, a much smaller creature; and the horses of the king's stables are said to have eaten each other.

The entry of Macduff allows Shakespeare to consolidate the first half of the play and to confirm that Macbeth has been named king and has already gone to Scone, the traditional place of coronation for Scottish kings, to be crowned. The imagery of this scene acts partly as a bridge between the first half of the play and the second. It recalls the first soliloquy of Lady Macbeth in Act I, Scene 5 ("Come, you Spirits"), and it foreshadows the language at the end of Act III, Scenes 2 and 3, concerning the murder of Banquo. The subplot of this second murder forms the basis of the whole of the next act.

Glossary

trifled (4) made trivial

travelling lamp (7) the sun

minions of their race (15) best of their breed

suborn'd (24) bribed

ravin (28) eat up

benison (40) blessing

Act III—Scene 1

Summary

Banquo suspects Macbeth but gains comfort from the second part of the Witches' prediction—that his own children will be kings. Having announced his intention to go riding with Fleance, Banquo is persuaded by the Macbeths to return later that evening to their new palace at Forres for a special feast. However, Macbeth realizes that the Witches' prophecy regarding Banquo represents a threat to his own position. Unable to endure the thought of Banquo's descendants claiming his position, Macbeth summons two hired murderers and confirms with them prior arrangements for the killing of Banquo and Fleance.

Commentary

Banquo's short soliloquy has two purposes: It reminds the audience of the details of the Witches' prophecy in Act I, and it reveals his own suspicion that Macbeth is Duncan's murderer. Ironically, his tone also recalls the ambitious tone of Macbeth in earlier scenes.

Macbeth and his wife make arrangements for the feast with all the confidence of their new rank. Note particularly Macbeth's adoption of the royal "we," The use of the plural in place of the singular pronoun is a traditional figure of speech by which the monarch expresses not only unity with his people but also his absolute authority over them. Banquo, once equal in status with Macbeth, acknowledges Macbeth's new position by addressing him throughout the scene as "my lord."

Style & Language

Other aspects of language confirm Macbeth's new status: strong verse rhythms, for example, appear in lines such as "Here's our chief guest" and "Fail not our feast." Macbeth's apparent disregard for time—of which he now has plenty—is clear in expressions such as "but we'll take tomorrow" and "But of that tomorrow." The word "tomorrow," like "hereafter," is full of irony in *Macbeth*. Tomorrow should be full of hope for the future, but the word comes back to haunt him later in the play. His use of the word here foreshadows the famous "Tomorrow and tomorrow" speech in Act V.

Even with his new title and robes of office, Macbeth does not feel entirely at ease: The security of his kingship rests partly on his own children's succession to the crown of Scotland. However, because he has no children of his own, his treacherous act of regicide—the murder of a king—appears pointless and has been committed on behalf of *Banquo's* promised successors. The soliloquy that Macbeth delivers is filled with the language of contrast. His split with Banquo is emphasized by opposing pronouns: "They hailed *him* father to a line of kings: / Upon *my* head they placed a *fruitless* crown, / And put a *barren* sceptre in *my* grip . . ." (60–62).

The line "To make *them* kings, *the seed of Banquo* kings!" (70) is almost incredulous, as if Macbeth is trying to convince himself that the Witches could not possibly have spoken the truth. Whereas Banquo still trusts in the fateful prophecy, Macbeth is all too ready to dismiss it. In Act I, Scene 2, the wounded captain reported that Macbeth the warrior-hero was prepared to disdain Fortune. Now Macbeth the murderer goes one step further by literally challenging Fate itself to a tournament (or "list"): "Rather than so, come, fate, into the list / And champion me to the utterance" (71–72). Note that the verb "to champion" here has its original meaning: to fight *against*, not *for*.

Character Insight

The entry of the hired murderers is a crucial element in the development of Macbeth's character. His use of others to do his dirty work presents him as politically powerful but morally weak. Long gone are the days when Macbeth would meet his enemy "front to front." Now he must commit murder with the seeming protection of distance— "something [distant] from the palace" (133). Shakespeare also contrasts ironically the murderers' pragmatic reaction to the idea of murder with Macbeth's conscience-stricken one.

The dialogue of the first part of the scene reveals that Macbeth has met the murderers before. Both then and now, he must convince them to work on his behalf. Whether true or not (we have no evidence), he kindles, or re-kindles, in them, a hatred of Banquo: "Know that it was he . . .," "This I made good to you in our last conference," "Do you find your patience so predominant in your nature that you can let this go?" The tone of these quotations is more than simply interrogative; Macbeth must ensure that the men are not persuaded by the slightest moral scruple, the slightest sympathy for Banquo, to betray the plan. Such a reaction would be entirely natural and human, but that humanity is precisely what Macbeth cannot now allow. Therefore, when the First Murderer replies, "We are men, my liege," Macbeth cuts off his speech and, in a sequence of powerful metaphors, reduces the humanity of these murderers to the level of beasts: "Ay, in the catalogue ye go for men, / As hounds and greyhounds, mongrels, spaniels, curs / . . . and demi-wolves are clept [called] / All by the name of dogs" (93–96).

Although Macbeth flatters the Murderers by suggesting that the business of Banquo's murder will elevate them above the common rank, his ironic tone reveals that he thinks of them as little more than beasts. Doubly ironic, then, is that this entire speech is admission to himself of his own inhumanity and imperfection: Macbeth himself is acting like a "demi-wolf." The lines are triply ironic when we see that indeed the murderers are, themselves, imperfect in carrying out his instructions for the "perfect" crime.

This notion of perfection is one that now comes to dominate Macbeth's thoughts. Banquo's death would make Macbeth's "health . . . perfect"; and the crime must be committed at "the perfect'st spy of the time" (the exact hour). Both of these quotations foreshadow Macbeth's line in Act III, Scene 4, when, hearing of the botched attempt to kill Fleance, he remarks "I had else been perfect." The tragic assumption that one can commit a perfect crime and escape the consequences is about to be tested.

As if to impress us with the connection between the killing of the king (the blame for which could, after all, be laid at the door of Fate) and the killing of Banquo (blame for which most definitely cannot), the final couplet ("It is concluded: Banquo, they soul's flight, / If it find heaven, must find it out tonight") ironically recalls the words spoken by Macbeth immediately prior to his killing of King Duncan: "Hear it not Duncan, for it is a bell / That summons thee to Heaven, or to Hell."

Glossary

verities (8) true predictions

parricide (31) murder of a parent

rebuked (55) mocked

fil'd my mind (64) defiled my guiltless conscience

rancours (66) bitterness

eternal jewel (67) immortal soul

Enemy of Man (68) the Devil

list (70) tournament

utterance (71) utmost

probation (79) approval

borne in hand . . . cross'd (79) deceived, double-crossed

half a soul (82) a half-wit

shoughs, water-rugs (93) rough-coated dogs

particular addition (99) a specific title

avouch (119) justify

Act III—Scene 2

Summary

This short scene allows the audience once more into the private thoughts of the murderous couple, while holding the action momentarily in suspense. As the hired killers make their way toward Banquo, Macbeth and his wife meet secretly. His wife attempts to soothe his troubled mind but ironically feels the same doubts herself. Killing the king has provided them with many more difficulties than they first envisioned. To the astonishment of his wife, Macbeth reveals his plan to murder Banquo.

Commentary

Dramatically and poetically, this scene precisely mirrors Act I, Scene 5. Then, Duncan's death was being plotted; now, the death is Banquo's (although Lady Macbeth is initially unaware of this). In the earlier murder, Lady Macbeth was most in command; in this murder, Macbeth is. Where formerly Macbeth was the one who needed convincing, now the weaker role passes to his wife. Macbeth's line "make our faces vizards (visors) to our hearts" recalls Lady Macbeth's earlier words "[t]o beguile the time, look like the time." Similarly, Macbeth's injunction to the spirits of darkness "Come, seeling night . . . " is an echo of the speech of Lady Macbeth's beginning "Come, thick night . . . .."

Despite Macbeth's personal bravado, neither he nor his wife seems entirely at ease. Lady Macbeth talks of her "doubtful joy" and Macbeth of his "restless ecstasy." In the world that the Macbeths have created for themselves, total peace no longer exists, and what has been achieved is only a half-measure. Even the dead King Duncan is able to achieve more totally what Macbeth never can: a respite from "life's fitful fever."

While Lady Macbeth appears to be looking back at the previous murder, Macbeth looks forward, anticipating the *next* murder, of which Lady Macbeth is not yet fully aware. That distinction between their two states of knowledge allows Shakespeare to play once more on the power relationship between husband and wife. Here, then is yet another reversal of character, and it is shown in two major ways: first, by Lady Macbeth's innocent-sounding questions and, second, by Macbeth's adoption of animal imagery. In Act I, Scene 5, Lady Macbeth was the one who spoke of "the raven" and "the serpent." Now Macbeth takes on the same language of horror, imagining his mind to be "full of scorpions," and speaking of the "bat" and the "shard-born (dung-bred) beetle."

The most powerful moments of the scene are the final ones in which Macbeth calls for the cancellation of the bond between himself and the world. "Bond" is more than simply a simile from the world of legal jargon. Just as Lady Macbeth earlier wanted to lose her sex, Macbeth now desires to be rid of his humanity. His direct connection with the natural world into which he was born threatens to keep him "pale" or fearful. A final point to make about these lines is the way in which the rhythmical stress falls unusually on the first syllable of the word "cancel":

"And, *with* thy *bloody and* in*vi*sible *hand*

*Can*cel and *tear* to *piec*es *that* great *bond* . . . ." (49–50)

Metrically, as well as dramatically, Macbeth is moving inexorably toward his tragic destiny. Meanwhile his wife, once so calm and collected, is losing that composure. Macbeth's line "Thou marvell'st at my words" suggests, like a stage direction, some moving response in her.

Glossary

scotch'd (13) injured

both the worlds (16) earth and heaven

foreign levy (25) foreign invasion

lave our honours . . . streams (33) show ourselves to be honourable by washing ourselves in acts of flattery

vizards (34) masks

Act III—Scene 3

Summary

The hired murderers meet as arranged. On hearing approaching horses, a signal is given, and Banquo and his son Fleance are attacked. The murderers' lantern is accidentally extinguished, and the job is left half-done: Although Banquo is killed, Fleance escapes.

Commentary

Appropriately, this scene takes place in the dark; the murderers carry lanterns and fail in their duty only when the light is accidentally knocked out and the entire stage is plunged in blackness. But this moment is also highly symbolic, foreshadowed at the end of Act II, when Ross remarks to the old man "By the clock 'tis day; / And yet dark night strangles the travelling lamp." In *Macbeth,* the forces of darkness seem constantly at odds with those of light.

In contrast to the dark, grisly nature of their job, the murderers' poetic speech is also comparatively light, particularly in the depiction of a traveler reaching the inn at sunset: "The west yet glimmers with some streaks of day; / Now spurs the lated traveller apace / To gain the timely inn" (5–7). One function of such poetry is to contrast the nature of word and deed. We have seen the same hypocrisy in Macbeth himself; he, too, is capable of poetry as well as murder.

Another function is to remind the audience of the existence of natural order and the possibility of salvation. In an ideal world, a belated traveler may hope to find "timely" accommodation, however late the hour. But in a world where the natural order of things has been inverted and in which light is extinguished, as it is symbolically in this scene, that hope is also extinguished. Banquo is riding not toward hospitable welcome but toward his own extinction.

Literary Device

The escape of Fleance is the turning point or *peripeteia* in Macbeth's tragedy. Banquo's dying words, ordering Fleance to "revenge," remind the audience of the Witches' prophecy to Banquo: that he will be father to a line of kings, even though he himself will not attain the throne.

Glossary

direction just (4) exact instructions

expectation (10) invitation

Act III—Scene 4

Summary

At Forres, Macbeth and his wife welcome the thanes of Scotland to the banquet. Immediately prior to the feast, one of the murderers appears at a side door and reveals to Macbeth the truth about the mission: their success in the killing of Banquo and their failure to murder Fleance. Macbeth recomposes himself and returns to the table. As he raises a toast to his absent friend, he imagines he sees the ghost of Banquo. As with the ethereal dagger, the ghost of Banquo appears to come and go, propelling Macbeth into alternating fits of courage and despair. Lady Macbeth invites the thanes to depart and, once alone, tries one last time to soothe her husband. But Macbeth's paranoid mind is already on to the next murder, that of Macduff. To ascertain his future with greater certainty, he makes clear his intention to visit the Weird Sisters once more.

Commentary

Macbeth's words and phrases to the thanes, such as "You know your own degrees" and "Both sides are even: here I'll sit i'th'midst" suggest a renewal of order and symmetry in Scotland, yet the audience knows that this is not the case. Both sides are not even, because Banquo is missing. Degree, or rank order, has been effectively perverted by Macbeth by his killing of the king and his usurpation of the throne. As in Act I, Scene 6, Lady Macbeth's words of introduction disguise her true feelings. Once again, the Macbeths act with suspicious confidence. This confidence is about to desert Macbeth, however, as his dark secret comes back to greet him in the form of the First Murderer.

At first, Macbeth is pleased with the murderer, telling him he is "the best," "the nonpareil" (without equal); moreover, Macbeth's own supposed invincibility is shown when he says that he feels "as broad and general as the casing air," but on hearing the unwelcome news that Fleance escaped his treachery, Macbeth's language abruptly changes: "But now I am cabin'd, cribb'd, confin'd, bound in / To saucy doubts and fears" (25–26). The alliteration of the hard *c* sounds reveals Macbeth's sense of constraint, in contrast to the freedom which he claims to have enjoyed previously.

The imagery of confinement and constraint plays an increasing part in his language from now on. For example, these words foreshadow the point in Act V, Scene 7 when, recognizing that he is physically trapped by the advancing English army, Macbeth cries out, "They have tied me to a stake, I cannot fly" (flee). Now, though, something altogether more terrifying holds him down and prevents him from moving: In the very place reserved for him at the table, Macbeth sees, or thinks he sees, the spirit of the assassinated Banquo.

The rich banquet, a symbol of great orderliness and generosity, now becomes a hellish parody of itself. Instead of Macbeth sitting "in the midst," dispensing his largesse as he would wish, his throne has been usurped by the bloody apparition of his former friend. Macbeth's language reflects this change. The ghost, so hideous that it would "appall the devil," appears to have risen from a grave or a "charnel-house." Macbeth cannot understand why what is dead should "be alive again," when its bones should "be marrowless" and its blood "cold." Finally, he challenges the all-too-real apparition to "dare me to the desert with thy sword."

In contrast to the urgent horror of Macbeth's addresses to the gruesome apparition are moments of comparative calm. Each time the ghost vanishes, Macbeth's relief is recorded in softer, more lyrical expression: "Can such things be / And overcome us like a summer's cloud, / Without our special wonder?" (112–114). Indeed, the entire structure of this scene shows a man swinging from one state of mind to another, recalling the structure of the earlier dagger speech. Three times Macbeth sees the ghost, and three times he appears to recover his senses. This alternating structure adds strongly to the impression of Macbeth's loss of control.

Lady Macbeth, on the other hand, remains constant in her judgement. Unlike Macbeth, she cannot see the ghost, and her tone is typically pragmatic and down-to-earth: "When all's done, / You look but on a stool." She appears to want to calm his rages, but anger simmers beneath her conciliatory words. Once more she upbraids her husband for his apparent lack of manhood. A specific parallel with the murder scene occurs when Macbeth accuses his wife of being able to "keep the natural ruby of your cheeks, / When mine is blanched (whitened) with fear" (116–117). Here, the words "ruby" and "blanched" clearly recall the distinction that Lady Macbeth made between the "red" hands of murder and the "white" heart of a coward (II: 2, 64).

With the departure of the guests, Macbeth appears to regain some of his earlier self-confidence. He announces his decision to visit the Weird Sisters once more, this time of his own accord. His language in this coda to the banquet scene is mysterious and prophetic: The short scene is dominated by the repeated word "blood" and by the idea that a tide of murder has now been initiated which Macbeth is powerless to stop.

Glossary

The feast . . . ceremony (35) Banquets which are given freely are made more attractive by the "sauce" of ceremony.

roofed (35) surmounted

flaws and starts (62) outbursts

become (63) suit

authoriz'd (65) written

maws (72) appetites

gentle weal (75) noble commonwealth

speculation (94) eyesight

protest me (104) claim that I am

disposition . . . owe (112) my own human nature, courage

augurs. . . blood (123) Prophecies have (in the past) revealed even the most well-hidden murders

magot-pies (124) magpies

fee'd (131) paid

wants (142) requires

Act III—Scene 5

Summary

Hecate, the classical goddess of the lower world who represents the spirit of ancient witchcraft, calls the weird sisters to her to complain that her own part in Macbeth's downfall has been overlooked and that she now wishes personally to make his downfall complete. The scene is unnecessary to understanding the play and was probably not written by Shakespeare.

Commentary

Hecate's supernatural spite is intended to echo that of the human dimension. She is a vindictive female spirit, whose forceful instructions to the Witches reflect the language of Lady Macbeth to her husband. Although unnecessary dramatically, the scene reinforces the philosophical question: Is Macbeth entirely to blame for his own downfall? In Hecate's opinion, he is. She tells the Witches that Macbeth "loves for his own ends" and prophesies that Macbeth "shall spurn Fate," recalling the words "disdaining Fortune" from Act I. Without this line of argument, it would be easier to suggest that Macbeth is powerless to control his own destiny.

Glossary

beldams (2) witches

Acheron (15) Hell

sleights (26) charms

security (32) overconfidence

Act III—Scene 6

Summary

Meeting with a rebel lord, Lennox reveals his doubts concerning Macbeth. His argument is that those who might be immediately suspected of murdering their kinsmen are less likely to have done so than Macbeth, who had killed the guards of Duncan's chamber so hastily. Although Lennox is prepared to accept Macbeth's actions, he cannot help feeling deeply suspicious of him. The other lord reveals to Lennox that Macduff has fled from Scotland to join forces with Malcolm in England. Moreover, they have requested help from England's King Edward the Confessor. Both Lennox and the other lord pray that God's vengeance may swiftly fall on the tyrannical Macbeth and that Scotland may return to peace once more.

Commentary

Some of the language of this scene is difficult. Its lines are full of pauses, half-spoken thoughts, and fragments of reported speech. Its function is twofold: first to convince the audience of Lennox's real thoughts about Macbeth. Even though Lennox appears loyal to Macbeth at the end of Act IV, Scene 1, here he divulges his concerns in lines such as "Men must not walk too late" and, more directly, the phrase "the tyrant's feast."

The primary function of the other lord is to confirm the news of Macduff's flight to England and to introduce the names of other rebel leaders, Northumberland and Siward, who will combine against Macbeth in the final act. But his words "That . . . we may again / Give to our tables meat, sleep to our nights" (32–34) also recall, ironically, the words of Macbeth to his wife in Act III, Scene 2: "But let the frame of things disjoint . . . / Ere we will eat our meal in fear, and sleep / In the affliction of these terrible dreams."

Glossary

marry (4) indeed

want the thought (8) help thinking

straight (11) straightaway

the two delinquents (12) that is, the guards of Duncan's chamber

an't (19) If

with Him above . . . work (33) with God's help

The cloudy messenger . . . clogs me with this answer The surly messenger refuses to report to Macbeth the news of Macduff's desertion for fear of punishment.

Act IV—Scene 1

Summary

Macbeth returns to the Weird Sisters and boldly demands to be shown a series of apparitions that tell his future. The first apparition is the disembodied head of a warrior who seems to warn Macbeth of a bloody revenge at the hands of Duncan's son Malcolm. The second is a blood-covered child who comforts Macbeth with the news that he cannot be killed by any man "of woman born." The third is a child wearing a crown, who promises that Macbeth cannot lose in battle until Birnam wood physically moves toward his stronghold at Dunsinane.

Encouraged by the news of such impossibilities, Macbeth asks, "Shall Banquo's issue ever reign in this kingdom?" The Witches present an image of a ghostly procession of future kings, led by Banquo. All this serves only to enrage Macbeth, who, trusting in his own pride, reveals in an aside to the audience his determination to slaughter the family of Macduff.

Commentary

This scene can be roughly divided into three: the Witches' casting of a spell; the supernatural answers to Macbeth's demands; and Macbeth's return to the cold world of political and social reality. The scene's structure deliberately recalls the opening scenes of the play. Once more, Macbeth's destiny is in question. Once more, he receives three prophecies. Once more, he is left on his own to decide how best to interpret those prophecies. And once more he fails to understand that Fate is inevitable, however he chooses to act.

The Witches' charm is fantastic: Its ingredients, thrown into a bubbling cauldron, are all poisonous. Moreover, these ingredients are all the entrails or body parts of loathed animals or human beings, which, taken together, can be interpreted as making a complete monster: tongue, leg, liver, lips, scales, teeth, and so on. The strong implication is that Macbeth himself is no longer a complete human being; he himself has become a half-man, half-monster, a kind of chimera.

Macbeth arrives at the Witches' lair with extraordinary boldness, knocking at the entrance in a way that ironically recalls the entry of Macduff into Macbeth's castle in Act II, Scene 3. When he "conjures" the Witches to answer him, his language is uncompromising: He matches their power with a powerful curse of his own, demanding to have an answer even if it requires the unleashing of all the elements of air, water, and earth; even if all the universe—natural or manmade—"tumble" into ruin. His most defiant act, by far, is to desire to hear the prophecy of his future not from the Witches, who are themselves only "mediums" of the supernatural, but from their "masters," that is, the controlling Fates.

Macbeth's demand is answered by a sequence of apparitions. Unlike the dagger and Banquo's ghost, these supernatural visions cannot be simply the workings of Macbeth's "heat-oppress'd brain." They are definitely summoned by the Witches. Once again, the audience is required to assess the extent to which Macbeth is responsible for his own actions. What is certain is Macbeth's response to each prophetic apparition: He appears to be super-confident, even flippant, in his replies. There is little fear or respect, for example, in his reply to the First Apparition: "Whate'er thou art, for thy good caution, thanks." And his punning reply to the Second Apparition's "Macbeth, Macbeth, Macbeth"—"Had I three ears, I'd hear thee"—displays a comic arrogance.

Apart from the first, all the apparitions, including the fourth and final one of a procession of future kings, contain children. The juxtaposition of children (pictures of innocence) and images of death, warfare, and blood, is dramatic and terrifying, but especially so for Macbeth: For a man who has no offspring, the image of children can only fill him with hatred and loathing.

Having rejected as impossible the second two prophecies, Macbeth asks for one last favor. The result appalls him, drawing all strength from him and reducing his earlier courage. The children who appear in this procession are the children of Fleance. The reflected light of their golden crowns "does sear (cut into) mine eye-balls" and causes his eyes to jump from their sockets. The climax to Macbeth's reaction occurs in the line "What! will the line (of inheritance) stretch out to the crack of doom?" in which he finally realizes the possibility of an entirely Macbethless future.

In a scene rich with special effects—thunder, ghosts and (possibly flying) Witches—Shakespeare adds a final visual stroke: The eighth child-king carries a mirror that reflects the faces of many more such kings. The effect of infinite regression can be achieved by looking at a mirror while holding a smaller mirror in your hand in which the reflection is reflected.

The Witches confirm the inevitability of what Macbeth has seen: "Ay sir, all this is so." There can be no equivocation, no argument, with Fate.

Emerging into the cold light of day, Macbeth seems immediately to forget the final prophecy, as he returns to the practicalities of what is increasingly a battle for his own political survival. On being informed that Macduff has fled to England, he announces his intention to wreak a terrible revenge on Macduff's wife and children.

Glossary

brinded (1) streaked

fenny (12) living in the marshes

howlet (17) young owl

yesty (53) frothing

lodg'd (55) beaten down

germens (59) seeds

farrow (65) litter of pigs

harp'd (74) guessed

impress (95) force

mortal custom (100) usual lifespan

crack of doom (117) Day of Judgment

antic round (130) mad dance

this great King (131) possibly a reference to James I (the king in Shakespeare's audience)

flighty . . . with it (145) Unless acted upon immediately intentions may be overtaken by time.

ACT IV—Scene 2

Summary

In Macduff's castle in Fife, Lady Macduff comforts and is comforted by her young son, who displays a courage beyond his years when confronted with the possibility that his father has turned traitor. Although warned by the Thane of Ross to escape before it is too late, Lady Macduff is encountered by Macbeth's henchmen, who brutally kill first her child and (as the audience learns in the following scene) her.

Commentary

This scene and the next should be considered together, for both deal with the question of treachery and loyalty, and both consider the nature of genuine courage, as opposed to the arrogant bravado of Macbeth.

Here is a woman apparently abandoned by her husband. She has been left to fend for her children like a mother bird in the nest. Even the tiny wren would show more spirited defense of her own family against a predator than Macduff has done, she argues. Her conclusion can be only that her husband "wants the natural touch"—that is, he lacks human kindness. It's interesting to hear in this phrase an ironic echo of the words of Lady Macbeth, who accused her husband of having precisely *too much* of "the milk of human kindness."

Ross' speech diverts Lady Macduff's justifiable anger away from her husband, whom he calls "noble, wise, judicious," toward the cruelty of the circumstances in which the country as a whole finds itself. The terror of Macbeth's Scotland is that no one can be sure of another's loyalty or treachery "when we are traitors, / And do not know ourselves; when we hold rumour / From what we fear, yet know not what we fear" (18–20).

Left on their own, Lady Macduff and her son converse further on the subject of her husband's loyalty. To her, Macduff has acted dishonestly, but her son, however naïve his view of the world, comforts her by his practical statement that the world is full of dishonest men. The entry of another messenger increases the urgency of the scene. Left on her own once more, Lady Macduff reflects, as Ross did, on the unpredictability and topsy-turvy nature of human society where "to do harm" is praiseworthy and to do good is dangerous.

Literary Device

The audience should not be surprised, given the direct and courageous speech of the young boy in his conversation with his mother, at the spirited defense he puts up against the murderers. His words ("Thou liest, thou shag-haired villain") foreshadow those of the brave Young Siward to Macbeth in Act V, Scene 7 ("Thou liest, abhorred tyrant") and remind us of the indomitable spirit of honor and justice that must ultimately prevail.

Glossary

coz (14) cousin

lime (34) bird lime (a sticky substance for trapping birds)

gin (35) trap

enow (56) enough

I doubt (66) I am concerned

savage (69) bold

fell (70) terrible

Act IV—Scene 3

Summary

In England, Duncan's son Malcolm tests the loyalty of his newest recruit, Macduff. By demeaning his own nobility and professing himself to be a greater tyrant than Macbeth, Malcolm hopes to goad Macduff into an open display of his loyalties. This attempt at reverse psychology has its desired effect. Macduff is thrown into a fit of anger against the "untitled tyrant" Macbeth, and Malcolm enlists his help in the struggle. When Ross appears with news of the slaughter of Macduff's family, Macduff is finally convinced not only to engage in the rebel army but also to take personal revenge upon Macbeth. This scene also includes a passage in which it is reported that England's king, Edward the Confessor, has provided more than political aid to Malcolm; he has been healing the sick by supernatural means.

Commentary

This scene develops further the important issues of loyalty and courage found in the preceding scene, and it is structured in two halves: the first concerns the testing of Macduff's loyalty by Malcolm; the second evokes the great passion of Macduff in the face of terrible grief and his sworn revenge on Macbeth.

It is helpful to think of this scene as a job interview. Malcolm begins by suggesting that Macduff may be prepared to betray him as "a sacrifice" to his previous leader, Macbeth. Macduff passes this stage of the interview by boldly announcing, "I am not treacherous." Still, Malcolm persists: Men may look as bright as angels on the outside but still harbor secret feelings within. Why, he asks, did Macduff desert his wife and children? At this point, Macduff nearly fails the test: He cannot believe that Malcolm is so short-sighted not to realize that his interests lie in defending not only his family but the whole nation of Scotland.

As in Ross' speech in Act IV, Scene 2, the context of this entire scene has been set in terms of the country as a whole: Macduff explains to Malcolm that "Each new morn . . . new sorrows / Strike heaven on the face, that it resounds / As if it felt with Scotland"(4–7). Later, Macduff cries out "O Scotland, Scotland . . . O nation miserable!" Macbeth's motivation in murdering Duncan may have been personal, but its effects have become very much public.

Malcolm's next move is a daring piece of reverse psychology: He claims that as a future king, he himself will be even more malicious and barbarous than Macbeth. To understand this scene, the audience must be aware from the start that Malcolm is lying when he suggests that he possesses no virtues, no nobility, no honor, and no qualities of kingship.

Macduff's response to this suggestion is at first cautious. His speech beginning with the words "Boundless intemperance in nature is a tyranny . . . " has a diplomatic tone. Macduff argues, probably against his better judgment, that certain human sins are forgivable, even in a king. Even avarice, the sinful desire for wealth, is "portable" when balanced against the good qualities of kingship. "But I have none," replies Malcolm, listing exactly those qualities which he *does* have and which, of course, Macbeth lacks. At this point, Macduff snaps. He cannot endure the thought that the country might have to undergo another reign even more vicious than Macbeth's. Seeing Macduff's clearly emotional response, Malcolm relents, revealing as fake the self-portrait he has previously given.

The next 20 lines may appear curious to a modern audience, for two reasons: first, because they were probably added as a flattering direct address to King James I, for whom the play was performed; and second because of what they reveal about the miraculous healing powers ascribed to his forebear, Edward the Confessor. According to legend, Edward had been able to cure scrofula, or the King's Evil, a glandular inflammation, simply by touching the diseased patient. But the passage is dramatically ironic as well: The king of England is shown to be a monarch of genuine goodness and to use the supernatural for beneficial purposes. Coming almost immediately after Macbeth's visit to the Witches, this contrast is made even more clear. Moreover, the speech introduces us to the choric (or commentating) figure of the Doctor, who speaks of disease but is powerless to cure the more severe, mental affliction of Lady Macbeth in the subsequent scene.

When Ross enters, his report consolidates this idea of disease. According to him, the entire country is "teeming" with illness: He reveals that "sighs, and groans, and shrieks . . . rent the air" and that "good men's lives expire before the flowers in their caps, / Dying or ere they sicken" (168–173). However, the worst news is for the ears of Macduff alone. In a piece of dialogue heavy with emotion, Ross relates the story of the murder of Lady Macduff and her little children. His speech wavers, as he tries to avoid telling Macduff the truth.

On hearing the news about his family, Macduff's reaction is understandable. Shakespeare gives him an implied stage direction in Malcolm's line "What man! ne'er pull your hat upon your brows," which suggests that Macduff must cover his face to prevent any unmanly show of grief. But Malcolm suggests that Macduff's tears should become "medicines . . . / To cure this deadly grief." Macduff, however, feels he can only blame himself. With ironic reference to his wife's words of the previous scene, he alludes to his "poor chickens," slaughtered by the "fell swoop" of a bird of prey. The emotional impact of this scene reaches its climax in Macduff's response when Malcolm tells him to "[d]ispute it like a man": "I shall do so / But I must also *feel* it as a man."

From this moment onwards, Macduff becomes the stereotypical avenging hero. It was he who first discovered the murder of Duncan, having arrived, Christ-like, at the gates of hell in Act II, Scene 3. Now he must take on himself the personal act of revenge. The scene is set for the final act.

Glossary

to friend (10) auspicious

recoil in an imperial charge (20) recoil (like a cannon) when under royal orders (from Macbeth)

jealousies (29) suspicions

afeer'd (34) confirmed

rich East to boot (37) all the wealth of the Orient as well

grafted (51) embedded

spacious plenty (71) at will

summer-seeming (86) youthful

foisons (88) abundance

interdiction (107) accusation

trains (118) tricks

detraction (123) self-accusation

convinces ... art (143) defeats all the attempts of (medical) skill

stamp (153) coin

eye (186) command

latch (195) catch

fee-grief ... breast (196) a personal sorrow

quarry ... deer (206) carnage of these dead creatures

Act V—Scene 1

Summary

Lady Macbeth has gone mad. Like her husband, she cannot find any rest, but she is suffering more clearly from a psychological disorder that causes her, as she sleepwalks, to recall fragments of the events of the murders of Duncan, Banquo, and Lady Macduff. These incriminating words are overheard by the Doctor and a lady-in-waiting.

Commentary

The staging of this scene is made clear by the first ten lines of the scene. The gentlewoman's description of how Lady Macbeth has sleep-walked in the past acts as a stage direction for the actress playing Lady Macbeth. Her agitated reading of a letter is of course a visual reminder of her reading of the fateful letter in Act I, Scene 5. More than this, Lady Macbeth is seen to rub her hands in a washing action that recalls her line "A little water clears us of this deed" in Act II, Scene 2. If these words are not enough to arouse the Doctor's suspicions, those that follow must suggest to him not only that she is suffering but also the reason for that suffering.

Character Insight

Lady Macbeth's speech has become fragmented and broken by an enormous emotional pressure: the suave hostess and cool, domineering wife has been reduced to a gibbering creature whose speech (almost) signifies nothing. There are no logical connections between her memories or her sentences, and indeed, the devastation of her mind is so complete that she cannot recall events in their correct order. For example, "Out damned spot" is followed by "The Thane of Fife had a wife," referring to Lady Macduff. Later we hear the line "Banquo's buried: he cannot come out on's grave," and finally she believes she hears Macduff knocking at the gate. It is as though all the individual murders have coalesced into one seamless pageant of blood. Perhaps the most ironic line is the one which near-perfectly echoes an earlier line of Macbeth's. When Lady Macbeth cries "all the perfumes of Arabia will not sweeten this little hand," we must not forget that she was not on stage to hear her husband's "Will all great Neptune's ocean wash this blood / Clean from my hand?" (Act II, Scene 2).

Lady Macbeth's line "What's done cannot be undone" not only reverses her earlier argument to her husband "what's done is done" (Act III, Scene 2); it also recalls the words of the general confession from the Prayer Book: "We have done those things which we ought not to have done, and there is no health in us." The Doctor agrees: In his opinion, Lady Macbeth needs a "divine,"—a priest—more than a doctor, reminding the audience of Macbeth's earliest doubts when he argues with himself before the murder of Duncan, "If it were done when 'tis done . . . we'd jump the life to come" (I:7,1–6).

Now, though, the promise of salvation has been all but abandoned. "Hell is murky," says Lady Macbeth, and that spiritual darkness is echoed by the fact that the scene is played entirely in the dark, with the exception of one candle, which Lady Macbeth insists on having next to her. She may be sleepless, but it is her soul's rest that really concerns her.

Glossary

accompt (37) account

practice (55) medical expertise

divine (71) priest

mated (75) amazed

Act V—Scene 2

Summary

Four lords of Scotland—Lennox, Menteth, Angus, and Caithness—resolve to join Malcolm and the English forces, who have by now marched into Scotland and are encamped at Birnam Wood, not far from Macbeth's stronghold at Dunsinane.

Commentary

This short scene develops the drama of the preparation for battle. In language that recalls that of Act III, Scene 6 and Act IV, Scene 3, the characters remind the audience of the various military alliances between Malcolm, England, and the rebel Scots. In this sense, the scene is simply a plot-filler, but there are three points to note: First, the audience is introduced once more to the fateful name of Birnam Wood, which the Third Apparition in Act IV, Scene 1 prophesied to be the downfall of Macbeth.

Literary
Device

Second, Caithness' portrait of Macbeth comes close to the description of a warrior-hero given by the Captain in Act I, Scene 2, especially in the phrase "valiant fury," but now the anger is not righteous: It arises from a "distemper'd cause" which Macbeth can no longer "buckle . . . within the belt of rule." Again, in another metaphor of clothing, Caithness adds that Macbeth's royal title "Hangs loose about him, like a giant's robe upon a dwarfish thief." (It is likely that nearly three centuries later, Robert Louis Stevenson was thinking of this line when he described the malicious dwarf Edward Hyde wearing the outsize clothes of the respectable Mr. Jekyll.) In Act I, Scene 3, Banquo talked of Macbeth's honors as "strange garments" which "cleave" (conform) to the shape of the body only by constant use. The metaphor is exact: Macbeth's title no longer *fits* him.

Third, the tone of the rebel Scots is one of uncompromising courage. Once more Scotland is described as a sick patient, the only cure for which is "each drop" of their own blood spilled in their country's defense.

Glossary

alarm (4) trumpet-call

excite . . . man (4) raise the dead

minutely (18) every minute

upbraid . . . faith-breach (18) rebuke his broken promises

dew (30) wet (with blood)

Act V—Scene 3

Summary

Macbeth dismisses reports of invasion by trusting to the prophecies of the apparitions, which seemed to promise him invincibility in battle. When a servant enters to announce the approach of a huge army, Macbeth appears momentarily to lose courage and then angrily spurns his servant and orders his armor to be put on. The Doctor, whose news concerning Lady Macbeth is just as grim, is treated with similar contempt.

Commentary

Macbeth's tone is typically brazen. The reports he has heard can have no consequence, given the prophecies of the three apparitions of Act IV, Scene 1. Throughout this scene, any doubts he may have are quelled by his bold imperatives: "Bring me no more reports," "Fly, false thanes," and more. We see a man completely self-assured, a "confident tyrant," as Siward calls him in the subsequent scene. These angry words do much to assert his own manhood, in contrast to the cowardice he perceives in others—not only his servant, whom he calls "cream-faced" and "lily-livered," but also the rebel soldiers, whom he insultingly refers to as "epicures" (that is, self-indulgent and lazy).

Literary Device

In the dialogue with the servant, Macbeth orders him to "prick his cheeks" in order to "put colour" back in his face, an ironic reminder of the earlier color symbolism when Macbeth was accused by his wife of having a white heart, as opposed to her own red hands. Another imperative—"Give me my armour"—has to be repeated when Macbeth's armourer, Seyton, initially refuses to do so. Similarly, when the Doctor confesses that he has been unable to cure Lady Macbeth's madness, Macbeth mocks his ability, challenging him to "Throw physic (medicine) to the dogs."

But there is also another Macbeth, who admits to being "sick at heart" and who feels he has entered the season of the "yellow leaf," that is, literally, the fall of his own reputation; and who, in a further moment of self-realization, recognizes the sickness of his own land: "If thou could'st, Doctor, cast / The water of my land, find *her* disease, / And purge it to a sound and pristine health / I would applaud thee to the very echo / That should applaud again" (50–54).

Earlier, referring to his wife's sickness, Macbeth has questioned the doctor's ability to remove from her those thoughts and feelings "Which weigh upon the heart." The Doctor's response: "Therein the patient must minister to himself" is particularly interesting. Where we expect "*her*self," Shakespeare instead uses the masculine pronoun, referring to a patient of either sex, particularly in proverbial statements such as this one. The suggestion is that Macbeth, too, must find the cure to his own disease. Macbeth's military preparation, which the Doctor says he has heard about, is unlikely to be any more effective than a medicinal preparation or remedy which *he* might prescribe for the sick nation of Scotland.

Glossary

English epicures (8) the self-indulgent English

sway (9) command

goose (12) cowardly

sere (23) dry

fain (28) rather

skirr (35) scour

oblivious (43) that brings oblivion

physic (47) medicine

cast the water (50) examine the urine (here, used metaphorically)

rhubarb . . . drug (55) purgatives

Act V—Scene 4

Summary

The English and rebel Scottish armies, under the leadership of Malcolm, meet at Birnam Wood. With military foresight, Malcolm orders each soldier to cut a branch and carry it in front of him as camouflage "to shadow the numbers of our host"—that is, to conceal the actual size of the advancing army.

Commentary

Literary Device

Malcolm's hope "That chambers (bedrooms) will be safe" in the future recalls both the location of King Duncan's murder and the motif of sleeplessness that runs through the play. Menteth's assured response—"We doubt it nothing"—is in heavy contrast to the "saucy doubts and fears" that have shaken Macbeth since even before the killing of Duncan and which will return to haunt him in subsequent scenes.

The order to each soldier to "hew . . . down a bough" as a leafy camouflage is taken direct from Holinshed's *Chronicles*; the aim is not to hide the advancing army but to confuse Macbeth as to the exact number of soldiers. Although Malcolm does not know it, his trick will not only fulfil the second of the prophecies of Act IV, Scene 1, but it will also play upon exactly the equivocation that has troubled Macbeth's mind since he first remarked (in Act I, Scene 3) that "nothing is but what is not."

Theme

In both Act V, Scene 2 and here, Macbeth's command over his few remaining followers is said to be based on constraint, not loyalty. His heartlessness is thus contrasted with the genuine feelings of loyalty which, it is implied, are felt towards Malcolm. In Act IV, Scene 3, Malcolm announced that Macbeth, like a rotten fruit, was "ripe for shaking"; now, according to Siward, "The time approaches," and in a final couplet adds "Thoughts speculative their unsure hopes relate / But certain issue strokes must arbitrate . . . (19–20). Once more, the impression is that the time for guesswork is over; certainty, and the assurance of goodness, must inevitably triumph over Macbeth's lack of it.

Glossary

constrained things (13) conscripts

just . . . event (14) righteous criticism awaits the outcome

Act V—Scene 5

Summary

Now fully armed, Macbeth confidently turns all his scorn on the advancing armies, only to find his brave rhetoric interrupted by an off-stage shriek. The queen is dead—whether by her own hand is not made clear—and Macbeth is left to contemplate a lonely future of endless tomorrows "signifying nothing." Yet another blow comes with the announcement that Birnam Wood appears to have uprooted itself and is even now advancing towards Dunsinane. Again Macbeth recalls the prophecies of Act IV, sure of, but still wishing to deny, their powerful truth.

Commentary

Style & Language

This scene, like Scene 3, starts with a bold imperative: "Hang out our banners on the outward walls." Macbeth's speech is warlike and defiant, his strength mirrored in that of the castle and men who surround him; his curse on the enemy vivid and graphic in its use of metaphor: "Here let them lie / Till famine and the ague (disease) eat them up . . ." (3–5). But the curse is empty rhetoric: In his play *Troilus and Cressida,* written two or three years earlier, Shakespeare had written that man's ambitious appetite for power, once it has preyed on everything in its path, can eat up only itself. Power-seeking tyrants tend toward self-destruction; if this curse falls on anyone, it's likely to be the curser.

At this point, Macbeth hears a heart-stopping scream. While a servant is dispatched to find the cause, Macbeth confesses in a brief soliloquy that such noises no longer have the power to frighten him. The audience recalls other noises: the owl-shriek that Lady Macbeth heard during Duncan's murder; the voice that Macbeth heard crying "Macbeth shall sleep no more!" and the fateful knocking at the door, all in Act II, Scene 2. But in a phrase that calls to mind the banquet scene (Act III, Scene 4), Macbeth admits that he has "supp'd full with horrors" and that his familiarity with slaughter means that such sounds can no longer amaze him.

The report of Lady Macbeth's death perhaps comes as no surprise, either to Macbeth or to Shakespeare's audience. The word "hereafter" recalls the "hereafter" of the Witches' first prophecy; their "hereafter" was the future that Macbeth was to inherit as king. But the word also refers, ironically, to the heavenly "hereafter," which Macbeth seems intent on denying for himself. In the hands of a sensitive actor or director, this exact word is what triggers the poetic outpouring on the nature of Time, which follows it.

The famous lines "Tomorrow and tomorrow and tomorrow" have a resigned, almost wistful tone to them, occasioned not only by the death of his wife but also by Macbeth's entire loss of purpose. Although there is perhaps an underlying bitterness at lost opportunity in the words "petty," "fools," "frets" and "idiot," for a man who has received such desperate news, this is not a desperate speech. In fact, compared with some of Macbeth's earlier "set pieces," its rhetoric is controlled, its metaphors precise: Time *is* like a path to "dusty death," and our lives *are* as "brief" as a candle. We *are* like shadows, or actors, on the stage of life. Again, the question occurs, as it did in Act I, Scene 7: How can a man who is capable of such poetic thought *act* as he does?

Macbeth's musings on this topic are cut dead by still another message, which reports what the audience already knows, the fulfillment of the second prophecy, the movement of the woods. Once again, Macbeth's response is both angry and reflective: "I . . . begin to doubt th'e-quivocation of the fiend— / That lies like truth . . ." (42–44).

To the servant, he must hotly deny the truth he has been told—to keep his public appearance and satisfy his own doubt—but he must also secretly accept the truth of the prophecy, even if logic persuades him that a moving wood is a lie. It is an understandably human reaction to such a paradoxical problem that Macbeth admits that he is literally stuck—"There is no flying hence, nor tarrying here" (48)—or, in his words from Act III, Scene 4, "Returning were as tedious as go o'er." On a psychological as well as a military level, Macbeth can neither move forward nor backward, neither advance nor retreat.

In this case, and with his gaze firmly fixed on the universe as a whole, Macbeth can only call, like King Lear, on the elements themselves: "Come wind, blow wrack!" he cries. It is the bold cry of a hopeless man.

Glossary

ague (4) disease

forc'd (5) reinforced

fell of hair (11) the hair on my flesh

treatise (12) tale

sooth (40) truthfully

estate of things (40) the physical frame of the universe

Act V—Scene 6

Summary

Malcolm and his troops have reached Dunsinane under the "leafy screens" of the branches, thus fulfilling the prophecy of the apparitions: Birnam wood *has* come to Dunsinane.

Commentary

Literary Device

The strong sense of movement and of impending threat is generated throughout Act V by the swift alternation of scenes. This, the briefest of all the scenes, at a mere ten lines in length, enables the audience to follow the advancing forces of Malcolm and England virtually to the walls of Dunsinane castle.

Theme

Two lines are worth commenting on: First, Malcolm announces that Siward, his "worthy uncle" shall lead the first battle, while Macduff and he complete the encounter "According to our order." The phrasing of this, with the implication that Siward is to be revered for his age and experience, establishes very strongly the idea of propriety and orderliness in Malcolm's army, in contrast with the comparative lawlessness and lovelessness of Macbeth's regime.

The second point occurs in the stirring final couplet, in which the trumpets sounding the advance are referred to as "harbingers of blood and death"; a *harbinger* is a sign of what is to come, a precursor of Destiny or Fate.

Act V—Scene 7

Summary

In a scene that foreshadows the final destruction of a tyrant in single combat, Macbeth is challenged by the courageous son of Siward. Immediately afterwards, Macduff is seen eagerly seeking out the man who was responsible for the murder of his family. Lastly, it is announced that Macbeth's forces have surrendered Dunsinane castle. But the business is not yet finished.

Commentary

The image of paralysis that ended Scene 5 is picked up immediately in Macbeth's image of himself as a baited bear. He is like a captured wild animal, furious yet unable to move: "They have tied me to a stake: I cannot fly." All he can do is to await his destiny. When a single figure enters, Macbeth must wonder, half-doubtful, whether his nemesis has arrived in the form of young Siward. The fight itself is preceded by a combat of words in which Siward appropriately taunts Macbeth with the words "devil" and "lie," words that have particular significance for his opponent. Macbeth's replies spur Siward into courageous but futile action. Before his exit, Macbeth gloats over the corpse of his assailant, with one final mockery: "Thou wast born of woman."

Literary Device

With ironic timing, the man who was *not* born of woman now takes Siward's place on the battlefield stage. The darkly vengeful figure of Macduff speaks of his obligation to the souls of his dead family: Revenge must be his and his alone if he is to escape his personal feelings of guilt at having abandoned his family.

Describing the surrender of Macbeth's castle, Old Siward (who at this point is ignorant of the heroic self-sacrifice of his son) explains that Macbeth's troops surrendered the castle with little resistance—"gently." Perhaps the audience recalls the "gentle" King Duncan, who, on his fateful visit to Macbeth's castle at Inverness in Act I, Scene 6, commented on the sweet air which surrounded it. Here, we feel that a weight has been lifted: the air will shortly "smell wooingly" once more.

Glossary

bruited (22) announced

rendered (22) surrendered

Act V—Scene 8

Summary

On another part of the battlefield, Macbeth and Macduff finally come face to face. Words, then sword thrusts are exchanged, and Macbeth, the bloody and tyrannical usurper of the throne of Scotland, meets his predestined end.

Commentary

As Macbeth ponders whether suicide, at this point, would be his better option, the avenging Macduff enters the scene with the bold challenge: "Turn, hell-hound, turn." Macduff's choice of the epithet "Hell-hound," recalling his earlier description of Macbeth as a "Hell-kite" (Act IV, Scene 3), confirms the true nature of the tyrant king. But in an equally bold rhetorical flourish, Macbeth warns Macduff that he is invulnerable, as "intrenchant" (uncuttable) as the air itself. Here, he mistakenly imagines that the words of the apparitions are a protective charm, which can keep him from physical injury.

Macduff takes an opposite view. Words alone, whether those of a ghostly prophecy or those of Macbeth himself, are nothing compared to his own word*less* anger: The true voice of revenge lies in action, not language. Furthermore, Macbeth should consider the circumstances of Macduff's birth. Macduff now reveals to Macbeth that he entered the world by being "untimely ripp'd" from his mother's womb: He was not, therefore, in the strict sense, "born" of woman. With the short but powerful sentence "Despair thy charm," Macbeth must know that his struggle for survival is over. The penultimate prophecy has come true.

Throughout the play, Macbeth has wondered about the veracity of the Witches' words: In Act I, Scene 3, he called them "imperfect speakers" because they had not told him all he desired to know; now he realizes that they spoke to him of his own imperfection. In the same scene, he admitted that their supernatural prophecy "Cannot be ill; cannot be good"; now he knows which was which. In Act IV, Scene 1, his opinion was that men were "damned . . . that trust them"; now he is damned by his own words. And in Act V, Scene 5, Macbeth spoke of his doubt concerning the predictions of "the Fiend / that lies like truth." Now he has no such doubt: "Be these juggling fiends no more believed / That palter with us in a double sense."

It is now Macduff's turn to mock Macbeth: He calls him "coward" and promises to have him publicly displayed—"baited with the rabble's curse" with a sign painted with the words "Here may you see the tyrant."

Glossary

intrenchant (9) uncuttable

the Angel . . . served (14) i.e. the Devil

cow'd (18) caused me to cower

juggling fiends (19) deceiving devils (or Fates)

palter (20) toy with

Act V—Scene 9

Summary

In the freshly taken castle of Dunsinane, events move to their natural conclusion. With the tyrant dead and war honors duly acknowledged, Malcolm is proclaimed by all the assembled thanes to be the new king of Scotland.

Commentary

This joyous scene is offset by its poignancy. Malcolm's opening line concerning those friends whom "we miss" is not only a gracious acknowledgement of what true loyalty means but also an indication of how he will rule in future, with the graciousness and humility that was associated with his father, Duncan.

A greater acknowledgement of human self-sacrifice comes in the report of young Siward's death, made more tragic by the fact that he was young ("He only liv'd but till he was a man") and that he predeceased his father, Old Siward. Nevertheless, Old Siward's response is one of great courage and faith. Asking whether his son was killed by a stroke to the chest or the back (in other words, whether he was facing or running from his opponent), Siward is told that he died "like a man," with his wounds "on the front." This account is enough to satisfy Siward that his son was "God's soldier"—a fitting and dramatic contrast with Macbeth who embraced the powers of evil so thoroughly.

Theme

Macduff enters the castle with the tyrant's decapitated head—like Claudius in *Hamlet,* the victim of his own poisoned chalice. The weight of these sad times has been lifted, and all that remains is for Malcolm to be acclaimed, in stirring fashion, as "King of Scotland." In his acceptance speech, the soon-to-be-crowned Malcolm invites his immediate audience to see him crowned at Scone, the traditional home of Scottish kings. The actions he will undertake as king will be performed " . . . in measure, time and place." This sentence carries a deep sense of unity and completion, reinforced by the rhyming couplet structure of the final four lines. Moreover, Shakespeare leaves us with the strong impression that the defining feature of future rulers (including James I of England) will be an acceptance of God's grace.

Glossary

go off (2) perish

unshrinking station (8) unyielding position

before (12) on his chest

compassed . . . pearl (22) surrounded by the elite of Scotland

CHARACTER ANALYSES

Macbeth

Macbeth is introduced in the play as a warrior hero, whose fame on the battlefield wins him great honor from the king. Essentially, though, he is a human being whose private ambitions are made clear to the audience through his asides and soliloquies (solo speeches). These often conflict with the opinion others have of him, which he describes as "golden" (I:7, 33). Despite his fearless character in battle, Macbeth is concerned by the prophecies of the Witches, and his thoughts remain confused, both before, during, and after his murder of King Duncan. When Duncan announces that he intends the kingdom to pass to his son Malcolm, Macbeth appears frustrated. When he is about to commit the murder, he undergoes terrible pangs of conscience. Macbeth is at his most human and sympathetic when his manliness is mocked and demeaned by his wife (see in particular Act I, Scene 7).

However, by Act III, Scene 2, Macbeth has resolved himself into a far more stereotypical villain and asserts his manliness over that of his wife. His ambition now begins to spur him toward further terrible deeds, and he starts to disregard and even to challenge Fate and Fortune. Each successive murder reduces his human characteristics still further, until he appears to be the more dominant partner in the marriage. Nevertheless, the new-found resolve, which causes Macbeth to "wade" onward into his self-created river of blood (Act III, Scene 4), is persistently alarmed by supernatural events. The appearance of Banquo's ghost, in particular, causes him to swing from one state of mind to another until he is no longer sure of what is and "what is not" (I:3,142).

But Macbeth's *hubris* or excessive pride is now his dominant character trait. This feature of his personality is well presented in Act IV, Scene 1, when he revisits the Witches of his own accord. His boldness and impression of personal invincibility mark him out for a tragic fall.

Lady Macbeth

Macbeth's wife is one of the most powerful female characters in literature. Unlike her husband, she lacks all humanity, as we see well in her opening scene, where she calls upon the "Spirits that tend on mortal thoughts" to deprive her of her feminine instinct to care. Her burning ambition to be queen is the single feature that Shakespeare developed far beyond that of her counterpart in the historical story he used as his source. Lady Macbeth persistently taunts her husband for his lack of courage, even though we know of his bloody deeds on the battlefield. But in public, she is able to act as the consummate hostess, enticing her victim, the king, into her castle. When she faints immediately after the murder of Duncan, the audience is left wondering whether this, too, is part of her act.

Ultimately, she fails the test of her own hardened ruthlessness. Having upbraided her husband one last time during the banquet (Act III, Scene 4), the pace of events becomes too much even for her: She becomes mentally deranged, a mere shadow of her former commanding self, gibbering in Act V, Scene 1 as she "confesses" her part in the murder. Her death is the event that causes Macbeth to ruminate for one last time on the nature of time and mortality in the speech "Tomorrow and tomorrow and tomorrow" (Act V, Scene 5).

Duncan

The king of Scotland should be a figurehead of order and orderliness, and Duncan is the epitome, or supreme example, of this. His language is formal and his speeches full of grace and graciousness, whether on the battlefield in Act I, Scene 2, where his talk concerns matters of honor, or when greeting his kind hostess Lady Macbeth in Act I, Scene 6. Duncan also expresses humility (a feature that Macbeth lacks) when he admits his failure in spotting the previous Thane of Cawdor's treachery: "There's no art to find the mind's construction in the face" (I: 4,11).

Most importantly, Duncan is the representative of God on earth, ruling by divine right (ordained by God), a feature of kingship strongly endorsed by King James I, for whom the play was performed in 1606. This "divinity" of the king is made clear on several occasions in the play, most notably when Macbeth talks of the murdered Duncan as having "silver skin lac'd with . . . golden blood" (Act II, Scene 3). The importance of royal blood, that is, the inheritance of the divine right to rule, is emphasized when, in the final scene, Duncan's son Malcolm takes the title of king, with the words "by the grace of Grace / We will perform."

Macduff

Macduff is the archetype of the avenging hero, not simply out for revenge but with a good and holy purpose. Macduff is the character who has two of the most significant roles in the play: First, he is the discoverer of Duncan's body. Second, the news of the callous murder of his wife and children (Act IV, Scene 3) spurs him toward his desire to take personal revenge upon the tyrannical Macbeth. When he knocks at the gate of Macbeth's castle in Act II, Scene 3, he is being equated with the figure of Christ, who before his final ascension into Heaven, goes down to release the souls of the damned from hell (the so-called "Harrowing of Hell").

Like Macbeth, Macduff is also shown as a human being. When he hears of the death of his "pretty chickens," he has to hold back his emotions. Even when (in Act IV, Scene 3) Malcolm urges him to "Dispute it like a man," Macduff's reply "I will do so. But I must also *feel* it as a man" enables the audience to weigh him against Macbeth, an unfeeling man if ever there was one. In the final combat between hero and anti-hero, this humanity is recalled once more when Macduff cries out, "I have no words; my voice is in my sword." It is his very wordlessness that contrasts with Macbeth's empty rhetoric.

Banquo

Banquo's role in the original source for *Macbeth* was as Macbeth's co-conspirator. In Shakespeare's play, he is depicted instead as Macbeth's rival; the role of fellow plotter passed to Lady Macbeth. Like Macbeth, Banquo is open to human yearnings and desires: He is, for example, just as keen to hear what the Witches have in store for *him* in Act I, Scene 3. He is kept from sleep by his dreams of the Witches (Act II, Scene 1). And in his soliloquy at the start of Act III, Scene 1—"Thou hast it now . . ."—there is more than a hint of resentment and, possibly, of the same naked ambition that leads Macbeth astray. Nevertheless, Banquo is a sympathetic figure for several reasons. First, he is ignorant of what the audience knows concerning the murder of the king and of his own impending doom. Second, he is a father whose relationship with his son is clearly an affectionate one.

Malcolm

With his brother Donalbain, Malcolm quickly ascertains the danger of remaining in Scotland and flees the country (Act II, Scene 3). By the time he reappears, in Act IV, Scene 3, he has won the support of Edward the Confessor (king of England), he has mobilized troops under Northumberland and Siward, and (to borrow a phrase from *King Lear*) he is "every inch a king."

If Macduff is the stereotypical revenger, Malcolm is the embodiment of all that is good in kingship, and this is seen particularly in Act IV, Scene 3, in which he tests the allegiance of Macduff. His testing of Macduff, although dramatically longwinded, is psychologically accurate. By pretending to be what he is not, he hopes to coax from Macduff a confession of his loyalty. This feature of his character—playing a part in order to strengthen the prospect of good—is in stark contrast to Macbeth, who plays a part in order to advance his own evil. In the final scene of the play, Malcolm is presented as the future king. His use of the phrase "by the grace of Grace" indicates the importance that he attaches to the service of good and reminds the audience of his direct descent from one who ruled by divine right, as opposed to Macbeth, who usurped the throne. Like his father Duncan, Malcolm is the representative of order.

CRITICAL ESSAYS

Macbeth on the Stage

Macbeth is one of Shakespeare's shortest and most intense dramas. Its straightforward plot and its strong characterization make it appealing for actors, directors, and audiences alike. The following brief discussion looks at the various theatrical contexts of the play from Shakespeare's time to ours.

Shakespeare's Theatre

The theater in Elizabethan and Jacobean times was basically a courtyard, surrounded on three sides by tall raised balcony areas. Other buildings in London, specifically public houses (taverns) and bear-baiting pits, were similarly designed. In a famous contemporary engraving of London, the Globe theater—where *Macbeth* was performed in 1611—is famously confused with the Bear-baiting pit. In this context, it is interesting to note Macbeth's lines (Act V, Scene 7) "They have tied me to a stake . . . but bear-like I must fight the course."

At the center and to the back of the courtyard was a raised stage, above which hung a depiction of the heavens—a blue roof, fretted with golden stars. The stage contained a trapdoor through which ghosts could appear and into which the souls of the damned could disappear. At the back of the stage was a curtain leading to the actors' dressing area—the *tiring room*.

The courtyard was open to the sky, so lighting was largely natural, but in some indoor theaters or palaces such as Hampton Court, where *Macbeth* was first performed in 1606 in front of King James I, candles were probably used to create an artistic tension between natural and "unnatural" (or artificial) light. Lady Macbeth has a candle "by her continually" in Act V, Scene 1, by which time natural light may well have already become gloomy. In fact, the numerous references to natural daylight and night-light in *Macbeth* make it a fascinating study for any historian of theater.

Shakespeare's play underwent several revisions during its lifetime. Specifically, the allusions to the Gunpowder Plot and the nature of kingship (Act IV, Scene 1) could have been added for the first performance in front of the king. What remains certain is that *Macbeth* has always been a highly visual and physical play: The apparitions, the references to parts of the body (hands, head), the fighting in Act V—all point to a play full of gesture and body language.

Modern Productions

As well as stage presentations, in recent years there have been a number of film adaptations, including *Macbeth* by Roman Polanski (1971) and *Throne of Blood* by Akiro Kurosawa (1957). Despite the play's bold outline, there are specific difficulties which any director must confront. The first of these is the role and staging of the supernatural elements of the play, specifically the Witches, the dagger, and Banquo's ghost.

The Witches are a vital component of the play because their prophecies in Act I, Scene 3 and Act IV, Scene 1 provide Macbeth with motivation for his actions. Banquo gives a hint as to their appearance when he refers to their chapped fingers, skinny lips, and beards; they need not, however, be costumed in the traditional form of the Halloween hag. They must have the capability of vanishing. Complex stage machinery in the Elizabethan theatre could have allowed them to "fly," but this is not necessary, because vanishing tricks can be performed in other ways, particularly by using a gauze curtain, which can be transparent or opaque depending on how it is lit. As an alternative, modern productions might also make use of visual projection or the voice-over.

The fact that the ghost of Banquo in Act III, Scene 4 has no lines means that it is frequently played in modern productions as simply a lighting effect, perhaps accompanied by a rushing of wind. This treatment reinforces Lady Macbeth's incredulity at her husband's reaction. She compares her husband's belief in Banquo's ghost with his faith in the earlier apparition of an "air-drawn dagger." A question therefore arises: Should *all* such effects be played invisibly to the audience? To do so may increase the psychological realism of the play, but it forces the audience to see Macbeth as a victim of hallucination. Such an interpretation may be confusing: After all, the *Witches* are real enough, because Banquo also sees them. Perhaps we only see the apparitions we want to see. If that's the case, we can reasonably assume that Macbeth must actually see a ghostly dagger as well as a ghostly Banquo.

The apparitions that the Witches conjure in Act IV, Scene 1 also require careful thought: The original stage direction for the third of these refers to a king carrying a looking-glass, and modern directors have had fun with this, employing several mirrors to create an infinite regression effect, for example. A final staging problem occurs with the appearance of Birnam Wood. Merely adding leafy camouflage to helmets does run the risk of looking rather silly.

The relationship between Macbeth and his wife—in particular the degree of responsibility which she has for the events of the play—is most important. Does her line "Unsex me here" make her chillingly asexual, or is she a heatedly sexual being whose relationship with Macbeth is more physical than intellectual? One thing is certain: Both Macbeth and Lady Macbeth must be able to move with ease between states of certainty and doubt. Her descent into madness and Macbeth's rapid swings between absolute self-knowledge and howling self-doubt are tests for any actor.

Major Themes of *Macbeth*

The ancient Greek notion of tragedy concerned the fall of a great man, such as a king, from a position of superiority to a position of humility on account of his ambitious pride, or *hubris*. To the Greeks, such arrogance in human behavior was punishable by terrible vengeance. The tragic hero was to be pitied in his fallen plight but not necessarily forgiven: Greek tragedy frequently has a bleak outcome. Christian drama, on the other hand, always offers a ray of hope; hence, *Macbeth* ends with the coronation of Malcolm, a new leader who exhibits all the correct virtues for a king.

The Fall of Man

Macbeth exhibits elements that reflect the greatest Christian tragedy of all: the Fall of Man. In the Genesis story, it is the weakness of Adam, persuaded by his wife (who has in turn been seduced by the devil) which leads him to the proud assumption that he can "play God." But both stories offer room for hope: Christ will come to save mankind precisely because mankind has made the wrong choice through his own free will. In Christian terms, although Macbeth has acted tyrannically, criminally, and sinfully, he is not entirely beyond redemption in heaven.

Fortune, Fate, and Free Will

Fortune is another word for chance. The ancient view of human affairs frequently referred to the "Wheel of Fortune," according to which human life was something of a lottery. One could rise to the top of the wheel and enjoy the benefits of superiority, but only for a while. With an unpredictable swing up or down, one could equally easily crash to the base of the wheel.

Fate, on the other hand, is fixed. In a fatalistic universe, the length and outcome of one's life (destiny) is predetermined by external forces. In *Macbeth,* the Witches represent this influence. The play makes an important distinction: Fate may dictate what will be, but how that destiny comes about is a matter of chance (and, in a Christian world such as Macbeth's) of man's *own choice* or free will.

Although Macbeth is told he will become king, he is not told how to achieve the position of king: that much is up to him. We cannot blame him for becoming king (it is his Destiny), but we can blame him for the way in which he chooses to get there (by his own free will).

Kingship and Natural Order

Macbeth is set in a society in which the notion of honor to one's word and loyalty to one's superiors is absolute. At the top of this hierarchy is the king, God's representative on Earth. Other relationships also depend on loyalty: comradeship in warfare, hospitality of host towards guest, and the loyalty between husband and wife. In this play, all these basic societal relationships are perverted or broken. Lady Macbeth's domination over her husband, Macbeth's treacherous act of regicide, and his destruction of comradely and family bonds, all go against the natural order of things.

The medieval and renaissance view of the world saw a relationship between order on earth, the so-called *microcosm*, and order on the larger scale of the universe, or *macrocosm*. Thus, when Lennox and the Old Man talk of the terrifying alteration in the natural order of the universe—tempests, earthquakes, darkness at noon, and so on—these are all reflections of the breakage of the natural order that Macbeth has brought about in his own microcosmic world.

CliffsNotes Review

Use this CliffsNotes Review to test your understanding of the original text and reinforce what you've learned in this book. After you work through the review and essay questions, identify the quote section, and the fun and useful practice projects, you're well on your way to understanding a comprehensive and meaningful interpretation of *Macbeth*.

Q&A

1. What do the weird sisters promise to Macbeth?

   a. the kingdom of Scotland
   b. everlasting life
   c. victory in battle

2. Why does Macbeth envy Malcolm?

   a. he is a better soldier
   b. he is the son of Duncan
   c. he has been named heir to the throne

3. What reason does Macbeth give for *not* killing Duncan?

   a. Duncan is his guest
   b. Duncan is his uncle
   c. Duncan is stronger than he is.

4. What does Lady Macbeth accuse her husband of being?

   a. a weak soldier
   b. a coward
   c. a bad king

5. Why do Malcolm and Donalbain flee?

   a. they are afraid they'll be accused of murdering their father
   b. they think that Macbeth will kill them next
   c. they want to join the English army

6. How does Macbeth persuade the murderers to kill Banquo?

   a. he says he will pay them

   b. he taunts them for their lack of manliness

   c. he threatens to execute them.

7. How does Lady Macbeth explain Macbeth's strange behavior at the banquet?

   a. that he is suffering from an illness

   b. that he has eaten "the insane root"

   c. that he has become obsessed with his new power

8. On returning to the Witches, what is the last apparition that Macbeth sees?

   a. a blood-covered child

   b. a procession of kings

   c. a procession of trees

9. How does Malcolm attempt to win Macduff's support?

   a. he tells Macduff about the slaughter of his family

   b. he claims he will be a better king than Macbeth

   c. he reveals that he has lied about his lack of kingly virtues.

10. How does Macduff receive the news of his family's murder?

   a. he is visibly upset

   b. he blames himself

   c. he vows to take revenge upon Macbeth

Answers: (1) a. (2) c. (3) a. (4) b. (5) a. (6) b. (7) a. (8) a. (9) c. (10) a, b and c.

Identify the Quote

1. All hail Macbeth, Hail to thee, Thane of Glamis

2. Come you spirits that tend on mortal thoughts, unsex me here

3. Glamis hath murdered sleep . . . .Macbeth shall sleep no more

4. Here lay Duncan, his silver skin lac'd with his golden blood

5. 'Tis unnatural, even like the deed that's done

6. I am in blood stepp'd in so far, that, should I wade no more, returning were as tedious as go o'er

7. What? Will the line stretch out to th'crack of doom?

8. But I have none, the king-becoming graces.

9. All my pretty chickens and their dam at one fell swoop?

10. Be these juggling fiends no more believ'd that palter with us in a double sense.

Answers: (1) [The Witches, speaking to Macbeth (and Banquo), reveal the first of their prophecies (I.3,48)]. (2) [Lady Macbeth, in a soliloquy, prays to the powers of darkness to deprive her of her femininity (I.5,40)]. (3) [Macbeth reports to Lady Macbeth these words that haunt his conscience (II.2.41)]. (4) [Macbeth, in the presence of Macduff, Lady Macbeth, Malcolm, Donalbain, Lennox and Banquo, justifying his killing of the guards of Duncan's chamber (II.3,109)]. (5) [The Old Man reveals his opinion to Ross. The normal behavior of the natural world has been turned on its head (II.4.10)]. (6) [Macbeth, to Lady Macbeth, planning the murder of Lady Macduff (III.4,135)]. (7) [Macbeth, expressing either rhetorically, or directly to the Witches, his fear that the royal line of Fleance will last an eternity (IV.1,117)]. (8) [Malcolm lies to Macduff in order to test his loyalty (IV.3,91)]. (9) Macduff responds emotionally to the news that the "hell-kite" Macbeth has swooped on his "nest" and killed his children and wife (IV.3,218)]. (10) [Macbeth finally realizes that he has misread his predicted Destiny (V.8,19)]

Essay Questions

1. Agree or disagree with the following statement: "*Macbeth* is a play about courage, which asserts the triumph of good over evil." In answering this question, you should remember that courageous acts are not always motivated by virtue.

2. Examine to what extent Lady Macbeth is to blame for her husband's downfall. Discuss the relationship between the couple as the play develops.

3. Discuss whether Macbeth is truly a tragic figure.

4. Some people suggest that the porter scene is included only so that the actor playing Macbeth has time to wash the blood off his hands. Do you agree? Or do you think the scene serves other purposes? Explain your answer.

5. From your reading, explain what Shakespeare imagined to be the qualities of a good king. How do Duncan and Macbeth fit this role? How might Malcolm do so?

6. Consider the use that Shakespeare makes of supernatural elements in this play. Be sure to include the Witches, the dagger, Banquo's ghost, the apparitions, and the Old Man's observations in your assessment.

Practice Projects

1. The Macbeth Murder Mystery: Write a short story in which the narrator is a detective who has been asked to investigate the deaths of Duncan, Banquo, and Lady Macduff. What are your hunches? And what evidence do you have to go on? You do not *have* to come to a conclusion.

2. The People v. Macbeth: Imagine that Macbeth does not die at the end of the play but is instead put on trial, and you are his defense attorney. Write your opening statement in this court case and present it to the class. Your class may choose to continue this exercise into a full court hearing with witnesses and expert statements.

3. Gunpowder, Treason, and Plot: Find out as much as you can about the Gunpowder Plot, the reign of James I, and the earliest performance of *Macbeth*. Design a colourful but accurate display for your classroom.

4. "Light thickens, and the crow makes wing to the rooky wood": Devise a theatre lighting plan for any one act from *Macbeth,* which will help to bring out the atmosphere of the play and enhance the supernatural and symbolic elements of the drama. (To approach this task, rule three columns on a page. In one column, show the Act and scene; in the next, indicate the line from the text on which the lighting is to change from one state to another; in the third, indicate the lights you would use. For example: Act I, Scene 7, Line 1; "If it were done . . ."; Single spotlight on Macbeth. Act I, Scene 7, Line 27; "How now"; lights full up.

CliffsNotes Resource Center

The learning doesn't need to stop here. CliffsNotes Resource Center shows you the best of the best—links to the best information in print and online about the author and/or related works. And don't think that this is all we've prepared for you; we've put all kinds of pertinent information at www.cliffsnotes.com. Look for all the terrific resources at your favorite bookstore or local library and on the Internet. When you're online, make your first stop www.cliffsnotes.com where you'll find more incredibly useful information about *Macbeth*.

Books

This CliffsNotes book provides a meaningful interpretation of *Macbeth* published by IDG Books Worldwide, Inc. If you are looking for information about the author and/or related works, check out these other publications:

Shakespearean Tragedy: Lectures on Hamlet, Othello, King Lear, and Macbeth, by A.C. Bradley, contains essays on the nature of Shakespearean tragedy in general and one essay on *Macbeth* in particular, with additional notes on Lady Macbeth's fainting and the question of Macbeth's children. New York: St. Martin's Press: 1967.

The Elizabethan World Picture, by E.M.W. Tillyard. Although it has only two brief references specifically to *Macbeth*, Tillyard's little book is, quite simply, the best aid to understanding philosophical, cosmological, and religious themes in Shakespeare. New York: The Macmillan Company, 1944.

Shakespeare on Film. Robert Shaughnessy, ed. This collection of essays explores film and video adaptations of Shakespeare's plays, including such topics as Shakespearean symbolism. Part of the New Casebook series. New York: St. Martin's Press, 1998.

Macbeth, edited by Alan Sinfield. This work offers more recent essays, several based on politics and gender, and includes Sigmund Freud's essay on the character of Lady Macbeth. Part of the New Casebook series. New York: St Martin's Press, 1992.

The Genius of Shakespeare, by Jonathan Bate, is a recent and popular book on Shakespeare. Its main interest is in the authorship question (who wrote Shakespeare's plays?) and the reputation of Shakespeare in the twentieth century. It is lucidly written and not specifically focused on any one play. New York; Oxford University Press, 1998.

It's easy to find books published by IDG Books Worldwide, Inc. You'll find them in your favorite bookstores (on the Internet and at a store near you). We also have three web sites that you can use to read about all the books we publish:

- www.cliffsnotes.com

- www.dummies.com

- www.idgbooks.com

Internet

Check out these Web resources for more information about William Shakespeare, *Macbeth,* and his other plays:

Mr. William Shakespeare and the Internet, http://daphne.palomar.edu/shakespeare/—Despite its unwieldy title, this is the best meta-index for Shakespeare resources on the entire Web. From here, you can jump to just about anything that has to do with *Macbeth* in particular and Shakespeare's work in general.

Enjoying Macbeth, http://www.pathguy.com/macbeth.htm—Autopsy pathologist Ed Friedlander guides you through a play that is clearly a personal passion for him. This site offers plenty of photographs, as well as bright and stimulating presentation. Most of what the site creator has to say about the play is accurate, but remember that sites like these are no substitutes for critical and scholarly essays.

Next time you're on the Internet, don't forget to drop by www.cliffsnotes.com. We created an online Resource Center that you can use today, tomorrow, and beyond.

Films and Other Recordings

Throne of Blood. Dir. Akiro Kurosawa. 1957. Shakespeare's play restyled as a mixture of Samurai history and Noh drama. The film plays up the supernatural side of the play, presenting a highly symbolic picture of tragic suffering.

Macbeth. Dir. Roman Polanski. 1971. A fairly accurate "contemporary dress" account, with some imaginative directorial additions.

Send Us Your Favorite Tips

In your quest for knowledge, have you ever experienced that sublime moment when you figure out a trick that saves time or trouble? Perhaps you realized you were taking ten steps to accomplish something that could have taken two. Or you found a little-known workaround that achieved great results. If you've discovered a useful tip that gave you insight into or helped you understand *Macbeth* and you'd like to share it, the CliffsNotes staff would love to hear from you. Go to our Web site at www.cliffsnotes.com and click the Talk to Us button. If we select your tip, we may publish it as part of CliffsNotes Daily, our exciting, free e-mail newsletter. To find out more or to subscribe to a newsletter, go to www.cliffsnotes.com on the Web.

INDEX

Q

Queen Elizabeth 4
quotes 94-95

R

regicide, 8
restless ecstasy, Macbeth, 45
revenge on Macbeth, 55
revenge, Macduff and, 62
revisions of play, 88
Ross, 13
royal we, Macbeth and, 41

S

sailor
    Macbeth comparison, 19
    weird sisters' curse, 19
savage, 59
Scotland king's coat of arms, 18
screaming and wailing voices, 37
screams, Macbeth's feelings, 72
servant of courage (Macbeth), 17
Shakespeare
    personal history, 2-3
    work of, 4
Shakespearean Tragedy, 97
Sinel, 21
Siward, 75
    died like a man, 80
    Macbeth and, 76
sleep
    Banquo, 32
    denied to Duncan, 19
    denied to Macbeth, 19
    murder'd, 19, 35
    pictures, 35
    sleeplessness, 7, 10
    sleepwalking, 7
    that chambers would be safe, 70
sleepwalking, Lady Macbeth, 64
soliloquy, 7
spells, Witches', 16
stage history of play, 7-8
stage productions of Macbeth, 89-90
stage psychology, dagger speech and, 32
starlight, cancellation and opposition of king
    and Macbeth, 23
strength of Lady Macbeth, 25
supernatural, King James I and, 8
synopsis, 10-12

T

technique, 9-10
Thane of Cawdor, Witches' prophecy, 20
Thane of Glamis and Cawdor, 12
Thane of Glamis, Witches' prophecy, 20
Thane of Ross, 18
The Elizabethan World Picture, 97
The Genius of Shakespeare, 97
theaters, 88
theatrical references, 9
this great King, 57
thread of a person's life, weird sisters and, 16
three-dimensional characters, 7
Throne of Blood, 98
Timber or, Discoveries, 4
tiring room, Globe theater, 88
trapdoor, Globe theater, 88
trapped animal, Macbeth as, 76

U

unnatural events, 37

V

Valour's minion (Macbeth), 17

W

washing hands, Lady Macbeth, 64
weather, Witches and, 16
Web sites, 98
weird sisters, 10, 16
    Banquo and, 20
    Banquo and prophecy, 41
    Banquo's reaction to, 32
    Hecate and, 52
    letter and prophecy, 24
    Macbeth knocking on door, 56
    Macbeth's return, 55
    Old Man's announcement, 39
    physical appearance, 19
    productions and, 89
    prophecies, 19
Witches 13. *See also* weird sisters
work of Shakespeare, 4

iffsNotes	The Call of the Wild & White Fang	Faust Pt. I & Pt. II	Julius Caesar
TERATURE	Candide	The Federalist	The Jungle
TES	The Canterbury Tales	Flowers for Algernon	Kafka's Short Stories
salom, Absalom!	Catch-22	For Whom the Bell Tolls	Keats & Shelley
e Aeneid	Catcher in the Rye	The Fountainhead	The Killer Angels
amemnon	The Chosen	Frankenstein	King Lear
e in Wonderland	The Color Purple	The French Lieutenant's Woman	The Kitchen God's Wife
the King's Men	Comedy of Errors…	The Giver	The Last of the Mohicans
the Pretty Horses	Connecticut Yankee	Glass Menagerie & Streetcar	Le Morte d'Arthur
Quiet on the Western Front	The Contender	Go Down, Moses	Leaves of Grass
s Well & Merry Wives	The Count of Monte Cristo	The Good Earth	Les Miserables
erican Poets of the 20th Century	Crime and Punishment	The Grapes of Wrath	A Lesson Before Dying
erican Tragedy	The Crucible	Great Expectations	Light in August
imal Farm	Cry, the Beloved Country	The Great Gatsby	The Light in the Forest
na Karenina	Cyrano de Bergerac	Greek Classics	Lord Jim
them	Daisy Miller & Turn…Screw	Gulliver's Travels	Lord of the Flies
tony and Cleopatra	David Copperfield	Hamlet	The Lord of the Rings
stotle's Ethics	Death of a Salesman	The Handmaid's Tale	Lost Horizon
I Lay Dying	The Deerslayer	Hard Times	Lysistrata & Other Comedies
e Assistant	Diary of Anne Frank	Heart of Darkness & Secret Sharer	Macbeth
You Like It	Divine Comedy-I. Inferno	Hemingway's Short Stories	Madame Bovary
as Shrugged	Divine Comedy-II. Purgatorio	Henry IV Part 1	Main Street
tobiography of Ben Franklin	Divine Comedy-III. Paradiso	Henry IV Part 2	The Mayor of Casterbridge
tobiography of Malcolm X	Doctor Faustus	Henry V	Measure for Measure
e Awakening	Dr. Jekyll and Mr. Hyde	House Made of Dawn	The Merchant of Venice
bbit	Don Juan	The House of the Seven Gables	Middlemarch
rtleby & Benito Cereno	Don Quixote	Huckleberry Finn	A Midsummer Night's Dream
e Bean Trees	Dracula	I Know Why the Caged Bird Sings	The Mill on the Floss
e Bear	Electra & Medea	Ibsen's Plays I	Moby-Dick
e Bell Jar	Emerson's Essays	Ibsen's Plays II	Moll Flanders
loved	Emily Dickinson Poems	The Idiot	Mrs. Dalloway
owulf	Emma	Idylls of the King	Much Ado About Nothing
e Bible	Ethan Frome	The Iliad	My Ántonia
y Budd & Typee	The Faerie Queene	Incidents in the Life of a Slave Girl	Mythology
ck Boy	Fahrenheit 451	Inherit the Wind	Narr. …Frederick Douglass
ck Like Me	Far from the Madding Crowd	Invisible Man	Native Son
eak House	A Farewell to Arms	Ivanhoe	New Testament
ss Me, Ultima	Farewell to Manzanar	Jane Eyre	Night
e Bluest Eye & Sula	Fathers and Sons	Joseph Andrews	1984
ave New World	Faulkner's Short Stories	The Joy Luck Club	Notes from the Underground
e Brothers Karamazov		Jude the Obscure	

CliffsN⏱tes™
@ cliffsnotes.com

Check Out the All-New CliffsNotes Guides

TECHNOLOGY TOPICS

PERSONAL FINANCE TOPICS

CAREER TOPICS